ONE WAY STREET?

Retrospectives on
Childhood Prostitution

ONE WAY STREET?

Retrospectives on Childhood Prostitution

MARGARET MELROSE, DAVID BARRETT AND ISABELLE BRODIE

A Voluntary Society of The Church of England and The Church in Wales

First published in 1999

The Children's Society
Edward Rudolf House
Margery Street
London WC1X 0JL

A catalogue record of this book is available from
the British Library.

ISBN 1 899783 27 X

Cover photograph modelled for The Children's Society.

Contents

FOREWORD   vii

EDITORIAL PREFACE   ix

ACKNOWLEDGEMENTS   xi

LIST OF TABLES   xii

1 INTRODUCTION   1
   Defining child prostitution   1
   Legal context of child prostitution   3
   The extent of the problem   5
   Social policy, poverty and prostitution   5
   Professional responses to child prostitution   8
   Difficulties with research   9
   Aims, methodology and ethics of the study   9
   The sample   12
   Gender and prostitution   12

2 WHO BECOMES INVOLVED IN
   PROSTITUTION?   15
   Family situation   16
   Sexual experiences   19
   Experiences of care and going missing   20
   Education   22
   Conclusions   23
   Summary   24

3 HOW DO YOUNG PEOPLE BECOME
   INVOLVED IN PROSTITUTION?   25
   When?   25
   Why?   27

How?   34
Summary   38

4 HOW DO YOUNG PEOPLE EXPERIENCE
   PROSTITUTION?   39
   Nature of involvement in prostitution   39
   First experiences in prostitution   40
   Violence   40
   Drugs   41
   Attitudes to the law and decriminalisation   42
   Earnings and age   47
   Views on penalties for men using young people   48
   Summary   48

5 WHAT MAKES YOUNG PEOPLE STAY
   IN PROSTITUTION?   50
   Money and work   50
   Drugs   57
   Friendships   59
   Stigma   61
   Summary   62

6 WHAT DO YOUNG PEOPLE THINK
   MIGHT HELP THEM TO EXIT?   64
   Factors facilitating exit for those still involved   64
   Leaving prostitution   67
   What might have prevented involvement?   71
   Family situations   72
   Facilitating exit   76
   Summary   77

7 IMPLICATIONS FOR POLICY AND PRACTICE   78
   Statutory and voluntary agencies   80
   The law and policing   83
   Education   84
   The labour market and welfare   86
   Key recommendations   87

APPENDIX   90

REFERENCES   92

Foreword

We all have much for which to be grateful to The Children's Society. In 1995 their report *The Game's Up* acted as a catalyst. It emphasised to us here in Britain that a problem many may have assumed had been consigned to history, or at least belonged to other cultures, was still present amongst us. The problem was that of child prostitution. The report confronted us with the unpalatable message that in the last decade of the twentieth century, despite the existence of the welfare state, post-war prosperity and humane legislation, sexual abuse and exploitation for gain were still blighting the lives of children, of both sexes. Worse, that the response of the legal and social agencies was, to say the least, less than adequate.

In *The Game's Up* there was much with which to agree; inevitably there was also much to question and develop. However, as a good report should, it prompted re-examination and action. The Association of Chief Police Officers produced its own guidelines, based on the premise that the children who were abused and exploited needed protection, while those who abused and exploited them should be pursued by the criminal justice process. In doing so the Police Service was not alone, for the Associations of Directors of Social Services and Chief Probation Officers, together with other representative groups from the voluntary and statutory sectors, either produced their own similar guidelines or supported those who did. To some it may not have been enough, but it was at least a start.

Valuable as that earlier work was, *One Way Street?* goes some considerable way in filling something of a void that has become evident over the years. Despite the recognition of the continued existence of the problem of child prostitution, despite the existence of new professional guidelines, and despite some recent valuable academic and social studies, there remains a need for more quantifiable primary research into the problem in this country. This is not simply of concern academically; it inhibits remedial action on the part of the investigative and caring agencies. It is not enough to agree that there is a problem and something must be done about it; there must be put in place the right programmes to give young people the freedom and support they need to leave prostitution. We know from experience elsewhere in the criminal justice system that effective strategies can be developed which significantly reduce the chances of children and young people offending or re-offending. The same must now be done for the victims of child prostitution. It will not be easy. As *One Way Street?* demonstrates, the impulses that ensnare children and young people are complex, and the subsequent exit strategies will need to be subtle and comprehensive. However, the significance of *One Way Street?* is that it identifies those impulses and influences. From this knowledge it must be possible for the caring agencies, both statutory and voluntary, to develop new ways of not only getting young people out of abuse through prostitution, but also making sure they stay out. Inevitably, not everyone will agree with all of the recommendations in the report, but that should not detract from the research and its findings. These should stimulate interest, debate and, I trust, action.

Some will find the stories of abuse and exploitation sad and depressing. That is understandable. In a civilised society even those not directly affected are diminished by child prostitution's continued existence; for those who are directly victimised it is a tragedy. But in these stories there is also hope. The experiences recounted in *One Way Street?* provide us with more information about child abuse through prostitution, and ultimately thereby point towards the solutions by which the problem can be tackled. For these further insights into this most pernicious problem we must thank the work's authors, Margaret Melrose, David Barrett and Isabelle Brodie, and once again, The Children's Society itself. Not least, we must thank those women and men, some of them very young indeed, who have been prepared to be so frank about their experiences to help and benefit others.

T.J. BRAIN
Deputy Chief Constable of Gloucestershire
Association of Chief Police Officers
Spokesperson on Prostitution

Editorial preface

In 1995 The Children's Society first brought the issue of children in prostitution to the notice of the public and uncovered a loophole in the law that allowed children to be punished for being abused through prostitution. We followed *The Game's Up* report with a book which looked at some of the practice issues for agencies involved. Police, health services, educationalists and the voluntary sector contributed chapters to *Child Prostitution in Britain: Dilemmas and Practical Responses*. At the same time we launched a deliberately confrontational campaign designed to raise public awareness of child prostitution in the UK.

This latest report builds on this successful work. The research set out to examine the reasons why children become involved in prostitution, the factors that keep them involved or help them to leave. We hope thereby to gain more understanding about how to prevent children from becoming involved in prostitution, and the services they need to help them escape their abusive lifestyles.

One of the most important changes the government could make is to restore benefits for 16- to 17-year-olds. Drug detoxification services are also urgently needed. We need more refuges and other street-based services for young runaways who make up such a significant proportion of young people involved in prostitution. We also believe it is counter-productive to retain a law which allows children to be prosecuted for selling sex.

It is vital to pursue the investigation and prosecution of those adults who abuse children through prostitution. Pilot schemes have already started to prosecute these offenders. By using child protection procedures, one police force amassed enough evidence in six months to charge nine adults with serious criminal offences including rape, unlawful sexual intercourse, attempting to procure a child for unlawful sexual intercourse, kidnap, unlawful imprisonment, witness intimidation and assault. Other prosecutions are pending.

One Way Street? shows that the issue of children in prostitution is a complex one, and initiatives to tackle poverty, loneliness and isolation must be far-reaching and truly inclusive if they are going to protect the young people who slip through the protective welfare net into the hands of abusive adults.

IAN SPARKS
Chief Executive
The Children's Society

Acknowledgements

The research team is indebted to all those who agreed to be interviewed as part of this study. We very much appreciate the willingness of participants to share their experiences with us, especially as this often involved recounting difficult and stressful aspects of their lives. We are also grateful to the projects which assisted us in accessing interviewees, and to the project workers who made such efforts on our behalf. Without such help it would have been impossible to carry out the research. Thanks are also due to The Children's Society for supporting the research and for making the necessary funding available.

The researchers would also like to thank colleagues in the Department of Applied Social Studies at the University of Luton, and in particular David Berridge, Professor of Child and Family Welfare, for his invaluable help and advice. Hartley Dean, Professor of Social Policy, Kathryn Ellis and Fiona Factor also provided important support. Margaret Melrose, as chief researcher on this study, would like to thank family and friends, especially Earl and Kris, for their emotional support throughout the fieldwork and writing-up for this study.

The Children's Society would like to thank the members of the Publications Advisory Group for their valued advice: Kathy Aubeelack; Nicola Baboneau; Ron Chopping (Chair); Annabelle Dixon; Sara Fielden; Judy Foster; Christopher Walsh.

List of tables

Table 1 Background of participants   15

Table 2 When and why participants first became involved
in prostitution   26

Table 3 How participants became involved in prostitution   36

Table 4 Participants' experiences in prostitution   39

Table 5 Participants' experiences of and views on the law   43

1

Introduction

It has been pointed out that 'juvenile prostitution is an area that is under-researched in Britain' (O'Neill *et al.*, 1995) and that 'young people's own accounts of prostitution' are relatively absent from the literature (Shaw and Butler, 1998). This study seeks to insert some of those voices and to restore this imbalance. It aims to further our understanding of the lived experience of these young people so that we may understand their needs and develop appropriate responses to them. In turn it should also provide information for agencies working in this area who are seeking to develop strategies to prevent child prostitution occurring.

This introductory chapter will provide a brief summary of what is known about young people's involvement in prostitution in Britain in relation to the following: definitions and extent of the problem; the legal context; the relationship between social policy, poverty and prostitution; and the responses of professional agencies. The chapter also describes the aims, methodology and ethics of the study, and issues of gender in prostitution.

DEFINING CHILD PROSTITUTION

The term 'prostitution' refers to a variety of activities 'performed under different terms and conditions' (O'Connell-Davidson, 1995). However, Shaw and Butler (1998: 181) offer a definition which they claim approximates 'to working definitions assumed by young people and street level workers themselves' and which actually echoes the useful definition provided by Green (1992):

> *'prostitution' is usually understood to mean 'the provision of sexual services in exchange for some form of payment such as*

money, drink, drugs, and other consumer goods or even a bed and a roof over one's head for the night'.

It has been widely accepted that there is a need to distinguish between adult and child prostitution (Jesson, 1993) and in recent years it has become more widely recognised, and accepted by many authors, that when we are talking about children and young people involved in prostitution, the problem is one of exploitation and sexual abuse by adults (Barrett, 1997; Swann, 1998; but see Shaw and Butler, 1998 for a different view on this).

McMullen (1987) has usefully argued that 'prostitution is an activity which describes a person's behaviour' rather than the person and although some writers in the field prefer the less pejorative term 'sex worker' to 'prostitute', others argue that this terminology is inappropriate when applied to children because it conceals the nature of the exploitation they suffer at the hands of adults (Barrett, 1997; Pitts, 1997). A majority of the people interviewed in this study chose the term 'working' in preference to 'prostitution' to describe what they do and this term, therefore, will also be employed in this report. As Shaw and Butler (1998) have acknowledged, very often young people do not associate their activities with what they think of as 'prostitution' and indeed one participant in the present study was quite adamant that she was *not* 'a prostitute':

> *I see myself as a working girl and don't actually class myself as a prostitute because I don't think that is the right word and I don't think that is the category that I come under because what I call a prostitute is a girl that will actually go out on the streets and sell her body for as little as £15 or £20 and go and get some heroin and go and get some crack, that's what I call a prostitute. I am not on drugs and I only sell my body to survive so I class myself as a working girl.*

In recent years our understandings of prostitution have expanded such that it is now recognised that it is a term which also encompasses the activities of boys and young men (McMullen 1987; Barnard *et al.*, 1990; West in association with de Villiers, 1992). Barnard's work with male 'rent boys' has shown that there are differences between men and women in the way that they practise in prostitution; in particular it was

found that young boys are less assertive than women in th̲ ̲
tions with clients (Barnard *et al.*, 1990). Our understandin̲g̲
boys and young men who become involved have also changed.
ous studies argued that rent boys were predominantly heterosex̲u̲al,
while more recent studies have argued that there was a certain amount
of homophobia informing these analyses (West in association with de
Villiers, 1992; Davies and Feldman, 1997) and have found that young
boys working in prostitution are frequently, although not necessarily,
homosexual.

McMullen (1987) provided a ground-breaking theoretical framework from which to understand juvenile prostitution based on his work
with young rent boys in Earl's Court, and more recently a theoretical
framework based on the idea of coercion by men, specifically the pimp
and the abuser, and termed the 'prostitution triangle', has been developed for understanding young girls involved in prostitution (Swann,
1998). O'Neill (1994, 1997) has contributed to this theoretical framework by demonstrating that prostitution occurs within a system of
male violence and male power.

LEGAL CONTEXT OF CHILD PROSTITUTION

The Children Act 1989 and the UN Convention on the Rights of the
Child define a 'child' as anyone under the age of 18 years and this is
the definition adopted in this report when 'children and young people'
are discussed.

There is a basic ambiguity in the laws relating to prostitution in
England and Wales, and for girls and young women 'prostitution' itself
is not illegal. Under the Street Offences Act 1959, however, it is illegal
for a 'common prostitute' to 'loiter' or 'solicit' for the purposes of selling sex. Under the same Act it is also illegal to live off immoral earnings, to run a brothel and to procure for the purposes of sex (Lee and
O'Brien, 1995; Aitchison and O'Brien, 1997; Adams *et al.*, 1997; ECP,
1997; Edwards, 1998). The law, however, does not make a distinction
between adults and children (Marchant, 1993; Aitchison and O'Brien,
1997; Edwards, 1998) and it is therefore, absurdly, possible for young
women who cannot in law *consent* to sex until they are 16, to be
charged and convicted for soliciting to *sell* sex from the age of ten
(Aitchison and O'Brien, 1997; Edwards, 1998). Indeed Home Office

statistics for 1995 show that 107 females under the age of 16 were cautioned (including two 12-year-olds and four 13-year-olds) and 29 convicted of soliciting in that year (Aitchison and O'Brien, 1997).

The legal position for boys and young men is different to that of girls and young women: in 1994 the High Court established that *'only women* can be charged with loitering under the Street Offences Act 1959' (Scambler and Scambler, 1997). For boys and young men involved in prostitution the Sexual Offences Act 1956 is applied. Under this legislation it is an offence for a man to 'solicit or importune in a public place for immoral purposes'. Just as the law does not distinguish between women and girls engaged in prostitution, it does not distinguish between men and boys and although, under the Sexual Offences Act 1956, a young man under the age of 18 cannot legally consent to sex with another man he may still be charged with 'soliciting or importuning' when under this age. Boys and young men are 'also likely to be charged with offences such as obstruction of the highway' (Aitchison and O'Brien, 1997).

The consequences of this are that there is no clear indication, from official statistics, of the numbers of boys and young men charged with offences which relate to prostitution. However, in 1995 official statistics reveal that three men under 18 were cautioned and four convicted for such offences.

In addition the law has also tended to criminalise and punish those who *sell* sexual services, whatever their age, rather than those who *buy* them (Adams *et al.*, 1997; ECP, 1997; Faugier and Sergeant, 1997; Shaw and Butler, 1998). It has consequently been argued that the current legal position is unjust and that child prostitution should be decriminalised; in other words, that recourse should not be made to the criminal law for young people who engage in prostitution. Instead, young people should be recognised as children and treated as children in need of protection under the Children Act 1989. However, this is a complex debate, and interested groups have adopted subtly different approaches, with some child welfare organisations emphasising the law concerning pimps and clients rather than that relating to young people. The Association of Chief Police Officers (ACPO) guidelines went some way to addressing the issue, in that they suggest that when young people are involved in prostitution they should be offered protection under the terms of the Children Act 1989, rather than punishment under the criminal law. These guidelines have not been universally adopted and, in any event, the guidelines allow for the criminal law to be applied in instances where young people 'persistently and voluntarily return to prostitution' (Brain, 1998). Consequently they do not support full decriminalisation. More recent Home Office guidelines, published towards the conclusion of the present study, also emphasise the need to focus on abusers and to treat young people working as prostitutes as victims (Home Office/Department of Health, 1998). However, this is an ongoing debate to which the generation of new empirical data, including the findings of this study, should contribute.

THE EXTENT OF THE PROBLEM

There is no consensus in the literature about the extent of young people's involvement in prostitution (McNeish, 1998). It is a 'hidden' population whose size is unknown and although estimates of prevalence are disputed (Shaw and Butler, 1998) it is thought that up to 5000 are involved at any one time (Thompson, 1995; Crosby and Barrett, 1999). Official statistics from the Home Office can contribute to our understanding of the scale of the problem, but there is still much work to be done in this area.

Recent pilot schemes of ACPO guidelines introduced by the police in Nottinghamshire and Wolverhampton, in which police respond to young people involved in prostitution by offering them protection under the Children Act 1989, rather than punishment under the criminal law, have shown that the problem in those areas is both more extensive and more complex than was originally thought (Brain et al., 1998). Certainly, in our study, the perception that more and more young people are becoming involved was shared by a majority of those interviewed. When asked if they thought more young people were involved now compared to when they first became involved themselves, over three-quarters said 'yes'.

SOCIAL POLICY, POVERTY AND PROSTITUTION

Over the past 20 years Britain has experienced an unprecedented rise in social and economic inequality (Hills, 1995; Barclay, 1995; Dean

with Melrose, 1998). In fact a report for the United Nations Development Programme (1996) found that inequality in the UK is 'now as
extreme as it is in Nigeria' (Townsend, 1996).

A report from the National Children's Bureau in 1994 identified 'a
trend towards sharply rising child poverty since 1979' (Wilkinson,
1994) and it has been estimated that 33 per cent of all children in the
United Kingdom now live in poverty (Oppenheim and Lister, 1996).
Children constitute 30 per cent of the poorest tenth of the population
but only 13 per cent of the richest tenth (Hills, 1995). This rise can be
attributed to global economic forces, the persistence of large-scale
unemployment and the hyper-casualisation of the labour market, combined with the introduction of various measures which have lowered
the real value of Income Support (Townsend, 1996:33).

The trends identified above have been paralleled by a growth in
youth unemployment and youth homelessness. It has been argued that
they help account for the growth and increasing involvement of young
people in various forms of informal economic activity ranging from
illegal or casual employment at one end, to street level economic activity such as drug dealing, begging and prostitution at the other (Bourgois, 1996; Jordan, 1996; Dean and Melrose, 1999). A UNICEF report
in 1993 contrasted a model of child welfare in Europe with a 'neglect
filled' Anglo-American model and warned that 'the swelling tide of
child neglect has potentially disastrous consequences' (Hewlett, 1993).

Evidence from various research studies shows that there is an unde-
niable link between poverty and prostitution (Andrieu-Sanz and
Vasquez-Anton 1989; Green, 1992; Groocock, 1992; Barrett, 1994,
1997; Edwards, 1992; O'Neill, 1994, 1997; O'Neill et al., 1995;
O'Connell-Davidson, 1995; O'Connell-Davidson and Sanchez-Taylor,
1996; Hardman, 1997; Pitts, 1997; Green et al., 1997) and that it is
'against a backdrop of social deprivation and unemployment' that most
women become involved in prostitution (Crosby and Barrett, 1999).
Other writers have explored the ways in which child-hostile social
policies (Mayall, 1997) contribute to young people becoming involved
in prostitution and prevent them from getting out once they are
involved (Green, 1992; Patel, 1994; Pitts, 1997; Green et al., 1997).

Though there are some exemptions, the Social Security Act 1988
withdrew income support payments to 16- and 17-year-olds, and levels
of benefit for those under 25 and unemployed have been greatly

reduced (Allbeson, 1985; Townsend, 1996; Green *et al.*, 1997; Dean, 1997; O'Neill, 1997). The consequence of these changes is that young people generally are 'significantly structurally disadvantaged' as they attempt to make the transition to adulthood and independent living (Coles, 1995). It has been argued that it is now almost impossible for 16- and 17-year-olds who are in conflict with their parents to live independently (Corby, 1997). Following changes to benefit regulations and hostel payments for young people, youth workers in Nottinghamshire noticed an increase in young people becoming involved in prostitution (Green, 1992).

The relationship between going missing from home or a residential institution and becoming involved in prostitution has been demonstrated by a number of studies in both Britain and Europe which have shown that young people are particularly likely to turn to prostitution as an economic survival strategy (Newman, 1989; Van der Ploeg, 1989; Rees, 1993; Stein *et al.*, 1994; Pitts, 1997). It has been claimed that 43,000 children under the age of 18 go missing from home or a care placement every year in Great Britain (Abrahams and Mungall, 1992) and there are concerns that increasing numbers are becoming involved in prostitution (Green, 1992; O'Neill, 1994; Green *et al.*, 1997; Pitts, 1997). Studies of young runaways have shown that young people are most likely to run away from areas which are characterised by economic stagnation, high unemployment and family poverty (Pitts, 1997). It has also been established that running away itself is bound up with other factors such as family conflict and sexual and/or physical abuse (Rees, 1993; Stein *et al.*, 1994; Crosby and Barrett, 1999).

A number of studies have highlighted the link between young women's involvement in prostitution and being looked after, particularly in residential accommodation (Kinnel, 1991; Jesson, 1991; O'Neill *et al.*, 1995; McNeish, 1998; Farmer and Pollock, 1998), though recent research suggests that only a small proportion of those who go missing overall from such locations become involved (Wade *et al.*, 1998). O'Neill *et al.* (1995) have provided a useful overview of feminist responses to young women involved in prostitution and of the experiences of young women in or leaving residential care. Research has also drawn attention to the inadequacies of social work responses to these young people (Jesson *et al.*, 1991), as well as to a lack of support and preparation when they are leaving care (Patel, 1994).

PROFESSIONAL RESPONSES TO CHILD
PROSTITUTION

As a result of the evidence produced from studies of young runaways,
The Children's Society undertook a study which looked specifically at
the issue of child prostitution (Lee and O'Brien, 1995). This suggested in particular that it was inappropriate to process these young
people through the criminal justice system. In 1997, The Children's
Society published an edited volume, *Child Prostitution in Britain:
Dilemmas and Practical Responses* (Barrett, 1997), which explored
responses to child prostitution from professionals in the youth service,
education service, police service, health service and the voluntary
sector. It also provided a number of recommendations in relation to
legal matters, education and central government policy. The police too
have examined the appropriateness of their own responses to this
problem (Brain *et al.*, 1998) and other writers have provided useful
analyses and case studies of voluntary and statutory agency responses
to this problem (Barrett, 1994a,b, 1995, 1997; Crosby and Barrett,
1999; Browne and Falshaw, 1998). They have recommended in particular that the best way to provide for the needs of these young
people is through street-based services which are in the vicinity of the
area in which they work. (The term 'work' will be used in relation to
prostitution throughout the report. This is derived from the fact that
participants in this study identified prostitution as their main job or
work.) However, these authors also argue that in the longer term it is
necessary to begin 'tackling issues such as social isolation, homelessness, lack of self-esteem, poverty, violence and sexual abuse' (Crosby
and Barrett, 1999). Browne and Falshawe (1998) urge the development of more outreach work and counselling services for these young
people. McNeish (1998) has provided a useful analysis of practitioners' perceptions of the problems confronting young people involved in
prostitution and has provided an insight into the types of responses
and interventions practitioners think would be useful for young
people.

Other writers (see for example O'Neill *et al.*, 1995, and Jesson,
1993) have argued that there is a need to know more about the lived
experiences of these young people if we are to develop effective and
meaningful responses to the problem of young people in prostitution.

Difficulties with research

Child prostitution is a very sensitive research topic and as with any such research it taxes the 'methodological ingenuity' of researchers (Lee, 1993). Shaw and Butler (1998) have acknowledged the practical difficulties of research in this area. They have argued that problems with definitions tend to create different estimates of the scale of young people's involvement and that difficulties with access tend to lead researchers and social workers to rely too heavily on 'unrepresentative agency populations' (Shaw and Butler, 1998:181). O'Connell-Davidson and Layder (1994) have provided an account of a study employing participant observation with women prostitutes. However, there appears to be nothing in the literature which discusses the emotional and/or ethical problems associated with doing research with/for this vulnerable group (but for a useful discussion of many of the relevant issues see Dean and Barrett, 1996).

Aims, methodology and ethics of the study

This study set out to explore with people who had become involved in prostitution when they were juveniles, the factors which these individuals saw as important in leading them into prostitution. It is therefore a *retrospective* study, which was undertaken using semi-structured interviews. It also sought to investigate with them the factors which they thought were important in preventing them from exiting from the lifestyle, and the types of interventions they thought might enable them to do so. In this sense the study aimed to learn from these young people rather than about them (Reinharz, 1992).

Participants were accessed through negotiation with projects which provide services for people working in prostitution at six different locations in England and Wales. Contact with these projects was, in most instances, facilitated by The Children's Society although its projects were not actually used for the research. A sample of 50 participants was achieved with the co-operation of participating projects. The sample is self-selected: i.e. people were approached by project workers and their 'informed consent' sought for participation in the research. They were assured confidentiality – and anonymity if they wanted it –

interestingly, most actually did not. However, in order to protect their confidentiality the names of all participants have been changed.

Six of the participants were still under 18 when the research was undertaken. This obviously raises some significant child protection issues and the question of the responsibility of researchers to participants. This possibility had been anticipated by the research team and it was decided that if those who were under 18 were currently in contact with a project which was providing them with support and help, then no further action should be taken and confidentiality could be offered in good faith. If, however, we had encountered a young person who was not in contact with appropriate services, then the relevant professionals would have been alerted.

The sample might also be described as a 'convenience' sample which has elements of randomness about it (i.e. the first 50 people to agree to take part were interviewed). The composition and characteristics of the sample are unavoidably determined by the nature of the projects through which participants were accessed. No claims can therefore be made about the statistical significance or 'generalisability' of the sample (or the data produced from it). The whole population of young people involved in prostitution is unknown and there are obvious and inherent difficulties with sampling 'unknown' populations (Lee, 1993; Dean and Melrose, 1996; Melrose, 1999). We are unable to state, therefore, the extent to which this sample might reflect the actual population of children involved in prostitution but we can say that their narratives give highly valid accounts of their reasons for becoming involved in prostitution, their difficulties with trying to exit from prostitution and the factors which they think might be important in enabling them to do so. The importance of such detailed, qualitative work should not be underestimated, and in this sense we might say that this is indeed a very useful sample which aims to explore young people's own accounts of their entry into and involvement in prostitution.

Participants were given £25 travelling expenses to participate in the research. It has been argued that such inducement may exert an undue influence and constitute a form of coercion on economically vulnerable people with the effect that it may distort the data (Homan, 1991). The propriety of compensating participants for giving their time to participate in research has been argued for elsewhere (Melrose,

1996, 1999) as has the notion that vulnerable groups are motivated to participate in research by a genuine desire for others to understand their situations and the factors which give rise to them (Melrose, 1996, 1999).

Financial incentives might be seen as an added advantage of participation in research but in our experience they are never the primary motivating factor. In a project such as this, where some of the participants might well be juveniles, financial compensation could be justified, at the very least, on the grounds that it 'saved' them from the streets for a period of time. Such payments are also increasingly becoming the norm in this area of social research. Projects were also offered, in total, a token payment of £25 for facilitating the interviews.

The approach of the study was interpretive and the main method employed was face-to-face semi-structured interviews. Most interviews were taped and additional notes were taken at the time of the interviews and a 'checklist' of main points, such as background, age of entry, reason for entry and so on, completed for each interviewee. The interviews were conducted over a three-month period, for the most part at projects or in homes, and relied on retrospective accounts of participants' entry into prostitution. Retrospective accounts have been criticised in the past for relying on memory which may be vague and/or imprecise and which may act as a 'filter' through which accounts are constructed (Shaw and Butler, 1998). However, in sensitive research (Lee, 1993) such as this they offer some advantages. Firstly, they avoid the ethical problem of needing parental consent to interview and secondly, emotional distance from traumatic events may be achieved with the passage of time and may therefore allow greater clarity in relation to them and make them easier to talk about (Wyatt *et al.*, 1993). There is also the obvious fact that one cannot explore a person's reason for entering prostitution with those who have not yet become involved. Retrospective accounts therefore offer an appropriate tool for exploring this issue.

The data obtained from interviews were coded using conventional data coding techniques and subject to analysis using the *Statistical Package for the Social Sciences (SPSS)*. While, as explained above, this was essentially an interpretive study, the mixing of qualitative and quantitative methods of analysis was found to be fruitful in generating an understanding of the data (see also Brannen, 1992).

THE SAMPLE

Fifty people took part in the research: 46 women and four men. They were accessed at six towns and cities across England and Wales. This indicates that prostitution is not just a problem confined to metropolitan inner city areas (McNeish, 1998). Approximately three-quarters (37) worked as street prostitutes while a small proportion (13) had combined 'streetwork' with 'working' from houses or flats. Over three-quarters (42) of the sample were white, three were of mixed parentage, three were Irish and two were African–Caribbean.

The ages of participants at the time of interview ranged from 14 to 56 years. Almost equal proportions were aged 25 and under (26), and over 25 (24) at the time of the interviews. For convenience, those aged 25 and under will be called the under-25 age group in this report. As noted earlier, six participants were aged under 18 (including one who was under 16), 21 were 18 to 25, nine were 26 to 35, 11 were 36 to 45 and three were 46 to 55. One participant was aged over 55. Almost half (22) had partners while almost two-thirds (29) had children. However, of those with children over half (17) did not have their children living with them; their children had either entered local authority care (nine) or were living with another family relative (eight).

The majority (approximately two-thirds – 33) of the participants had interrupted or prematurely terminated educational careers. Many had a history of truancy and/or exclusion from school. Some said they had simply 'stopped going' to school, in some cases from as young as 12.

Approximately a third (16) of the sample were currently housed in council or housing association accommodation, just over a fifth (11) were private tenants, eight were living in hostel accommodation and nine were living in 'other' housing situations. Amongst these there were some who still lived with parents, an owner–occupier and some who constitute the 'hidden homeless' – people staying with friends and sleeping on sofas or floors (Douglas and Gilroy, 1994).

GENDER AND PROSTITUTION

Although the legal context of prostitution is different for males and females and research reveals that there may be differences in terms of working practices (Barnard et al., 1990), this study found no noticeable differences between males and females in terms of the factors which led them into prostitution and the factors which they found made it difficult to get out. In view of the fact that the number of men in the sample was so small, it makes no sense to analyse the data in terms of gender differences. However, to avoid subsuming the experience of men entirely under the experience of women a few points will be made here about the men in the sample. It is important to stress that this was a very small group, and that it would be very problematic to generalise from their experience.

All the men interviewed had been involved in prostitution from an early age: two began when they were 13 and two when they were 14. At the time of the interviews one man was 18, one was 20, one 25 and one 26. All were white and at the time of the interviews two were still involved in prostitution while two had exited. The two who had left prostitution had done so because they had been diagnosed as HIV positive. Two men identified themselves as homosexual although one did not identify himself with the 'gay scene' and was 'straight acting'. Two identified themselves as heterosexual. Two were involved in relationships, one heterosexual and one homosexual. Two had a history of being looked after and one a history of going missing while being looked after. Two had a history of going missing from home while one had been thrown out of his home by his father when he was 14 when he revealed that he was gay. He had had no contact with his father in the intervening 12 years.

Two of the men had interrupted or prematurely terminated educational careers, one did not speak about his educational background and one had a university degree. Two of the men said they did not use drugs – although one of these admitted that he drank rather excessively. One had been using drugs before becoming involved in prostitution, while one had started using drugs after involvement in prostitution because he found 'it made the work easier'.

All the men said they first became involved in prostitution on a 'freelance' basis – that is, they made the decision on an individual basis, though it was not necessarily their desired option. Two of the men said they adopted prostitution as a 'survival strategy', i.e. to provide for basic needs for food and shelter, while running away from or having been forced to leave the parental home. One became involved because he wanted money for drugs and the other because he wanted money for things he couldn't otherwise afford. One of the men who became involved in the context of being on the run described prostitution as 'a quick, fast and easy way of making money'.

Two of the men reported having been physically abused in their homes and another one reported that he had experienced conflict in the home. Two of the men reported that they had been sexually abused by people outside the home – one had been raped when he was 13 years old. None of the men had been convicted or cautioned for prostitution-related offences. Three of the men were in favour of 'decriminalising' prostitution for those over 18 and one was in favour of 'decriminalisation' for those over 16.

CHAPTER 2

Who becomes involved in prostitution?

Previous research has shown that family discord, sexual abuse, running away from home or care or both, experiences of residential care, homelessness and poverty are significant features in the lives of young people who become involved in prostitution (Shaw and Butler, 1998; McNeish, 1998; Green *et al.*, 1997; Pitts, 1997; O'Neill *et al.*, 1995; Lee and O'Brien, 1995; Jesson, 1991, 1993; Kinnell, 1991) and that it is difficult to disentangle their involvement from such factors (Crosby and Barrett, 1999). These features were also found to be highly significant elements in the lives of many of the people interviewed for the present study. The main features of their background experiences are summarised in Table 1 below.

Table 1 *Background of participants (n=50)*

Experiences of conflict/abuse in family	36
First sexual experience in context of abuse	21
Experience of being looked after	24
History of going missing from care	14
History of going missing from home	26
History of going missing from home and care	10
Disrupted educational career	33

In this chapter we will explore their family backgrounds, their experiences of being looked after by the local authority ('in care'), their experiences of going missing from home, care, or both, and their educational experiences.

FAMILY SITUATION

Nearly three-quarters (36) of the people in the study had experienced conflict or abuse in their families. Of these, half had been physically or sexually abused in the home. Only half (9) of those who suffered abuse at home had been looked after by the local authority.

Susan was 16 and, as a result of conflict with her stepfather, was in voluntary care when she first became involved in prostitution. She was 26 at the time of the interview and still involved in prostitution. She described the sort of abuse she had experienced as a child and told us that she has 'anger outbursts' and,

> *I can't control myself when that happens. I think one of the reasons I've got this problem is maybe because of what went on in my childhood and stuff like that. For example, my stepfather locked me in a room about half the size of this room we're sat in now and there used to be a mattress in it and a bucket and that bucket was my toilet and I was left to do me business in that bucket and I could never go out anywhere. He used to lock me up continuously twenty-four hours a day. The only time I used to be let out was when I had to go to school or when I went downstairs to have something to eat. That's the only time I got let out of the room and it was not just me that got locked up in that room, it were me two-year-old sister as well.*

Lorraine, who was 18 at the time of the interview, told us she had been 'physically, sexually and mentally' abused by her mother 'from the age of three' and when her mother subsequently re-married she was abused by both her mother and stepfather from the age of eight until she became looked after when she was 12. She had become involved in prostitution when she was 17 after she had been violently raped. When asked about her reasons for becoming involved she said,

> *Men take sex anyway. I was self-destructing and I thought it was all I was worth.*

Kate, who was 18 years old, addicted to heroin, pregnant and still involved in prostitution at the time of the interview, had experienced a great deal of conflict with her mother when she lived at home because her mother had 'give me up' to be looked after by her grandparents when she was six years old. She returned to her mother's when she was 12 but started running away because she felt that her mother didn't really want her. She explains,

I were living with me gran in [place] and I didn't like it there and I wanted to come back to [place] but me mum didn't want to take me back. She like, she totally ignored me all the time.

Kate's full story is given below.

Kate
Age at time of interview: 18
Age of entry into prostitution: 12

Kate is a heroin addict – she has been using it since she was 14 but said she has had a 'habit' since she was 16. At the time of the interview Kate was pregnant and still involved in prostitution.

When Kate was six her mother said she was 'out of control' and sent her away to live with her grandparents. Her siblings remained with her mother in the family home. She says her grandparents were good to her but that she didn't want to be there. She wanted to be at home with her mum.

When she was 12 she returned to live with her mother but her mother wouldn't or couldn't answer her questions about why she had been sent away to her grandparents in the first place. This caused a lot of arguments between Kate and her mother. Kate was running away from home and truanting from school. She says everyone around her was 'doing stuff that wasn't right'.

One day when she was 12 her friend asked her if she would come with her to her uncle's house. When she got there she realised it wasn't an uncle at all. The man they went to visit asked Kate to take her clothes off for him. She thought he just wanted her to strip so that he could look at her but once she had stripped he asked her to perform oral sex and paid her £30 for doing it. She said she was 'scared' and 'embarrassed' on this first occasion but it seemed like 'easy money'.

Kate was intermittently involved in prostitution between the ages of 12 and 14. At 14 because her mum 'didn't want her' she went to stay with a friend of hers, a woman who was 'right nice' to her and whom she 'looked up to'. She started using heroin at this time and became more fully involved in prostitution although she didn't work every night, 'just when I felt like it'. She and her friend worked together for a few weeks but then the friend's boyfriend started taking her money. Kate returned home to live with her mother for a short time before leaving again because of constant arguments and Kate's feeling that her mother didn't want her anyway.

She expressed a lot of resentment towards her mother, mainly because she felt her mother had never satisfactorily explained why she had sent her away to her grandparents. She said she was tired of people telling her to stop blaming her mother for ruining her life. She said she had had a social worker 'but I just weren't interested'. Although the social worker knew that she was involved in prostitution, it was never really discussed. Kate felt that all they ever talked about was her relationship with her mother. Her mother knew that she was involved in prostitution at 14.

When she was asked about what she thought might have helped her, Kate said she wanted her mother to try to stop her being involved in prostitution, but she never did. She felt that now her mother 'isn't responsible' for her they get on better.

Kate has a boyfriend now and is looking forward to having a baby to love: 'I won't do to this baby what my mum did to me'. She was asked if her boyfriend was going to support her when she got to the stage of pregnancy when she would no longer be able to work in prostitution. She looked a little incredulous and said, 'But if he goes grafting he'll only end up in prison and where will that get us?' When she was asked if she intended to carry on 'working' until she had the baby she said, 'I've not got much choice, have I? It's either that or be sick'. She went on to explain that if she did not have heroin the baby would also be sick and she would risk a miscarriage.

Kate feels that she is unable to hold down a 'normal' job because of her 'habit'. When asked how she feels about her circumstances and life at present, she said, 'Fucked. It's fucked, innit?'

Almost a third (15) of participants came from families in which they had experienced stepparenting and almost a fifth (eight) lived in households where their parents had divorced. Though one should be cautious in assuming a direct relationship, the entry of a new adult often seemed to bring additional conflict into households. Many participants related that there were conflicts between them and their stepparents and even, on several occasions, that the natural parent was forced by the stepparent to choose between them and the child. As Sue told us,

My mum has actually been married twice, she's had two marriages, both marriages are broken through alcohol and abuse and stuff like that. I actually got put into care when I was 15 years old and my stepfather, my mum's second husband, give my mum a choice: it was either him or me. So she picked him and put me into voluntary care.

SEXUAL EXPERIENCES

Almost half the sample (21) reported that their first sexual experience took place in the context of abuse and just over a quarter (13) of all participants reported that they had had their first sexual experience before they were ten years old. Four participants reported that their first sexual experience took place in the context of prostitution.

Melanie was 34 at the time of the interview and 14 when she first became involved in prostitution. Following an argument with her father, he had told her to leave the house at this age and she had nowhere to go. Melanie has four brothers and she is the middle child. She was sexually abused by her oldest brother for as far back as she can remember. She thinks she was about three when it started and her brother was about ten or eleven. When she was about five or six Melanie's godfather, who used to look after her while her parents were working, started sexually abusing her and he would give her money. As a result of this she says, 'You could say I've been a prostitute since I was seven'. Melanie had never been looked after. Melanie's full story is given on pp. 69–70.

The above findings suggest that there is much family conflict and abuse which goes undetected. Indeed, as Browne and Falshaw (1998) have shown, there is a 'dark figure' of sexual and violent crimes against·children which do not appear in the official statistics. Indeed, the majority of victims of child abuse are never identified. Estimates vary considerably, but some studies of prevalence of sexual abuse of children suggest that as many as one in ten are sexually abused at some point in their childhood (Corby, 1997). The findings reported here do indicate that young people's entry into prostitution is 'inextricably linked' to abuse, family discord and poverty (Crosby and Barrett, 1999).

EXPERIENCES OF CARE AND GOING MISSING

Previous studies have drawn our attention to the links between the experience of residential care and entry into prostitution (Kinnel, 1991; Jesson, 1991, 1993; O'Neill, 1995; Farmer and Pollock, 1998). This is a complex relationship and does not mean that residential care is, in itself, the direct cause of prostitution. It is important to remember that a very high proportion of young people entering residential accommodation will already have experienced difficulties at home and different forms of abuse (Berridge and Brodie, 1998; Sinclair and Gibbs, 1998). Some may, indeed, become looked after as a result of concerns about their sexual behaviour.

In this study, almost half (24) the participants had experienced local authority care at some point in their lives. The majority of these had lived in residential accommodation although the ages at which they first entered care and the time they spent there varied greatly across the sample. Of those who had been looked after, just over half (14) had a history of going missing from care. A recent study has shown that going missing while looked after is in fact quite common, though the numbers of those becoming involved in prostitution as a result of this are quite small. In the 12-month period in which the research was conducted, 43 per cent of all 11- to 16-year-olds looked after by four local authorities went missing at least once, while nearly half the sample (46 per cent) had first gone missing from home (Wade *et al.* 1998).

The study found that it was the youngest members of the sample who had most frequently experienced the care system. This in itself serves as an indicator of the serious nature of their problems. Over half (15) of those who were under 25 at the time of the interviews had been looked after at some point in their lives compared to just over a third (nine) of those who were over 25. Almost two-thirds (eight) of those who were 18 and under at the time of the interview had been looked after. This group had also become involved in prostitution at the youngest ages. In the whole sample, over half (13) of those who had been looked after had become involved in prostitution before they were 14. Amongst those who had not been in public care just over a third (nine) became involved in prostitution before they were 14.

Just over half the sample (26) had a history of running away from home though only a third of these had experienced the care system. Slightly over half (14) of those who had been looked after had a history of going missing from care. A minority of ten participants had a history of going missing from both home and care. However, just over a third (19) of the entire sample said they became involved in prostitution when they were on the run. Also, it was those who were over 25 at the time of the interviews who said most frequently that they became involved in prostitution in order to survive while on the run.

The study also found that it was those with a history of going missing from home or residential accommodation who tended to become involved in prostitution at the youngest ages. Almost three-quarters (ten) of those with a history of going missing while looked after became involved in prostitution before they were 14 but a smaller proportion – two-thirds – of those who had a history of running away from home became involved at this age. However, we found that it was those who had a history of running away from *home*, rather than residential accommodation, who most frequently said they became involved in prostitution while missing.

Rachel, who was 18 at the time of the interview but no longer involved in prostitution, was 14 and living at home when she first became involved. She described her difficulties at home:

I was 14 years old the first time I started working and I wasn't very happy with my family because my dad left me when I were eight years old. I lived with my mum at the time [when she first became involved] *but I kept running away from home because my mum's boyfriend used to beat me up and . . . there always used to be family arguments.*

Rachel went on to tell us that 'I went through a hard experience with my father' and then disclosed,

I was raped by my real father when I was about six years old. But I forgive him for it because – well I don't know why really but I just – I ain't seen him for ten years and I miss him and I love him to bits.

Rachel went into care when she was 15 because her mother 'needed a break' and they both decided it was 'the best thing to do'. She told no-one about her father's abuse until two years ago when she told her mother, but,

She didn't believe me so I left it.

Lesley became involved in prostitution at 13 when she was running away from residential care where she had been placed because her mother was unable to cope with her. She was 40 and no longer involved in prostitution at the time of the interview. She told us,

I was brought up by my mum, my granny and my grampa. My granny died when I was seven years old. My mother was an only child and she wasn't very well equipped to deal with me. My grampy died a couple of years later, so consequently I was in and out of children's homes when I was young.

When she was asked about how she first became involved in prostitution, Lesley said,

I was in children's homes. I run away ... quite frequently [laughs] and I got to meet a group of young people in [place], similar young people, and obviously when you run away I was staying ... and then one of my friends just said one day, 'Well, you know, you've got to start earning your living now, Lesley'.

Lesley's full story is given on pp. 33–4.

EDUCATION

In addition to their experiences of disruption, discord and abuse in their homes, the majority of participants (33) had experienced interrupted or prematurely terminated educational careers as a result of truancy, bullying and/or exclusion from school. This had in itself exposed them to greater risk and, additionally, many did not therefore possess qualifications appropriate to the demands of the labour market. As Rachel told us,

> *I left school because I couldn't cope with being bullied at school. I didn't care any more so I walked out of school when I was about 15. I couldn't concentrate because of all the stuff I had on my mind; ye know, my mum's boyfriend and family arguments and stuff and people bullying me.*

CONCLUSIONS

The testimonies of Susan, Linda, Kate, Melanie, Lesley and Rachel and the evidence presented above confirm findings from other research that disruption, abuse, family conflict, residential care, running away and problems with school are significant features in the lives of young people who become involved in prostitution. The experiences of these young women go some way to support the contention that experiences of early sexual abuse are 'at least a strong pre-disposing factor towards subsequent prostitution' (Shaw and Butler, 1998) and that young people experiencing abuse and/or conflict are likely to try to escape it by running away from home and/or care (Stein *et al.*, 1994) but that the act of running away itself exposes them to more risks and dangers and makes them vulnerable to exploitation through prostitution (Lee and O'Brien, 1995; Green, 1992; Barrett, 1997; Pitts, 1997; Crosby and Barrett, 1999; Farmer and Pollock, 1998; Shaw and Butler, 1998). In fact Strauss (1994) has claimed that in order to support themselves half of runaway children resort to prostitution, stealing, drug dealing or other crimes after just one month on the run.

However, while the experience of public care is an important element in the accounts of some of those interviewed in this study, it appears that a substantial proportion of young people who run away and become involved in prostitution have not come through the care system even though they may have experienced conflict and/or abuse in their homes. This suggests, therefore, that care leavers, runaways and those who suffer violence and abuse early in their lives are by no means the only young people who adopt prostitution as a survival strategy.

The findings presented here urge us to understand these personal circumstances of abuse, conflict and running away and involvement in prostitution within the wider socio-economic and policy context outlined in the introduction. They also suggest that there is an ongoing need for all professionals to be alert to the possibility of abuse and the importance of effective child protection systems.

SUMMARY

- A significant number – 36 – of the people in this study had experienced conflict or abuse in their early lives.

- The seriousness of the family and educational problems of many participants is further highlighted by the fact that almost half had been looked after.

- Those with a history of going missing from home or care became involved in prostitution at the youngest ages.

- Over half of those who had been looked after had a history of going missing.

- The majority of participants had interrupted or prematurely terminated educational careers and therefore tended not to possess formal qualifications or skills appropriate for the labour market.

CHAPTER 3

How do young people become involved in prostitution?

As we have seen in the previous chapter, it is predominantly those children and young people who have experienced family conflict and abuse, who have been looked after ('in care') and/or gone missing from home or residential accommodation who become involved in prostitution. In this chapter we will explore the 'when', 'why' and 'how' of their entry into prostitution; that is, the ages at which they became involved, the factors which propelled them into prostitution and the mechanisms through which they became involved.

WHEN?

Just under two-thirds (32) of participants first became involved in prostitution before they were 16, and three-quarters of these (24) actually became involved when they were 14 or younger. Two of these first became involved when they were 11. In the whole sample the average age for first involvement was 14.5 years; for boys it was slightly younger than this (13.5 years) and for girls the same (14.5 years). The most frequently cited age for first involvement was 15 while the ages at which people first became involved ranged from 11 to 17 years. Around two-thirds of the sample therefore became involved in prostitution before they could legally consent to sex.

The motivations for entering prostitution were complex and varied, and often involved more than one reason. As we have seen in the previous chapter, it was those children who became involved in the context of being 'on the run' who tended to enter prostitution at the youngest ages, and over half (13) of those who became involved aged 14 or younger said they did so because they needed money to survive while they were on the run. These individuals had nowhere to live and no other source of income. However, a third (eight) of those who first became involved at 14 or before said they did so because they wanted money for things they could not otherwise afford. As has already been discussed, the majority of this younger group had experienced conflict or abuse in their families and a high proportion had a history of going missing either while living at home or while being looked after in a children's home. Ten of those who became involved while on the run had been abused, in contrast to only three of those who became involved because they wanted money for items they could not otherwise afford.

A slightly higher proportion of the under-25 age group became involved aged 14 or younger compared to the over-25 age group. Half the younger age group (13) became involved at this age compared to just under half of the older age group (11). This is despite the fact that those in the older age group said slightly more frequently that they became involved in the context of going missing from home or a care placement.

It is clear from this evidence that many young people enter prostitution before they are legally old enough to enter the formal labour market or to receive welfare benefits in their own right. Given these circumstances it is clear that many see themselves as facing choices which lie within a range of illegal options such as theft, begging, shoplifting, robbery or prostitution.

Table 2 summarises the ages at which people first became involved and their reasons for doing so.

Table 2 *When and why participants first became involved in prostitution (n=50)*

When	Involved in prostitution before 16	32
	Involved in prostitution before 14	24
Why	Adopted prostitution as a survival strategy	18
	Became involved because they wanted money for things they couldn't afford	18
	Became involved because they wanted money for drugs	7

WHY?

In the whole sample approximately three-quarters (36) of the participants said their main reason for becoming involved in prostitution was
a lack of money. Of these half (18) adopted prostitution as a 'survival
strategy' and the other half said they wanted money for things they
could not otherwise afford. These items were typical of usual adolescent desires, such as trainers and fashionable clothes.

PROSTITUTION AS A SURVIVAL STRATEGY

We heard in the previous chapter from Lesley who explained how she
became involved when she was running away from children's homes
and for whom prostitution was a means of survival. She told us,

> That's how I lived. To survive. I didn't go back home then [at 13].
> From that age I managed to survive myself. You know, doing my
> own thing and getting along. By the time I was 15 I had a place of
> my own . . . it was just something you did. You had to live so you
> did it.

Lesley's full story is given on pp. 33–4.

PROSTITUTION AS A SOURCE OF INCOME

On the other hand, Lisa, who was 18 at the time of the interview and
still lived at home with her mother, who apparently didn't know about
her involvement in prostitution, had first become involved when she
was 12 and saw prostitution as a means of providing things she wanted
to do or buy but could not afford,

> Well, I started when I was about 12 and nearly 13. Umm, I never
> lived with my dad, just lived with my mum. Went to school and
> that, as you do sometimes, and then like I start . . . cos I was
> maturer than everyone else I started going to clubs and that and I
> needed money, so, easy way.

Susan, who we have heard from above and who had been in voluntary care when she first became involved in prostitution, explained
why she needed money,

> When I first went into care when I was 15, nearly 16, with me

*only being in voluntary care the local authority was not prepared to
give me any money to survive because I was on voluntary care. I
wasn't on a court order or anything like that so I had to get money
in my own way. So that's how I got into it.*

Jenny, who became involved at 15 and was 17 at the time of the
interview and still involved in prostitution, describes how for her, the
temptation of money was difficult to resist,

*It was a bit funny really. I'd always hung around with the girls,
d'ye know what I mean? Stood talking to them on the corner and
punters would stop me and I wouldn't be interested. And then
one day I were out, drinking, and I was walking through* [known
local beat] *eating a kebab and this punter, an Asian guy, stopped
me and he was pressuring me all the way up the top* [of the road]
*and he went all the way up to £75 for oral but I kept saying 'no'.
He went right up to £115 then he said he wouldn't go any higher.
So that were it. I just did it and ever since then I just worked. But
it hasn't been as easy as that really.*

That the lack of money prompted the majority of the sample to enter
prostitution correlates with evidence from other research which
demonstrates that poverty is strongly related to entry into prostitution
(Green, 1992; Edwards, 1992; O'Neill, 1994, 1997; O'Neill *et al.*,
1995; Barrett, 1992, 1994, 1997; Pitts, 1997; Hardman, 1997; Green *et
al.*, 1997; Crosby and Barrett, 1999). However, the over-25 age group
tended to say more frequently than those under 25 that they had
adopted prostitution as a 'survival strategy' – half of the older group
gave this reply compared to approximately a quarter of the younger
group. On the other hand, just over a quarter of those over 25 said they
had become involved in prostitution because they wanted money for
things they could not otherwise afford compared to almost half of the
under-25 age group.

Of the small proportion of participants (14) who did not cite money
as their main reason for becoming involved in prostitution, half said
their main reason was to get drugs or the money to provide drugs.
Most of those who gave this reply were in the under-25 age group.

Dawn, who was 24 at the time of the interview and 16 when she had
first become involved in prostitution told us,

I had a baby when I was 15. His dad was violent. I stayed with him . . . till [child] *was about four. But all that time he was beating me up, being violent. When I was 16 I was going out, saying I was just going out with me friends but I was going out working, getting money. Got on heroin, got addicted to heroin, I was feeding mine and his habit that's why I was going out . . . I did it really cos of me heroin addiction . . . Really I just did it like to feed me heroin habit.*

DRUGS AND OTHER REASONS

A fifth (five) of the younger age group said they wanted drugs or the money to buy drugs. High levels of drug use have been found amongst those involved in prostitution in other studies (Crosby and Barrett, 1999; Curren and Sinclair, 1998; Crosby, 1997; Plant, 1997; McKeganey and Barnard, 1990; Faugier *et al.*, 1992; Faugier and Sergeant, 1997; Kinnell, 1989; Blom and van den Berg , 1989) and they have found that it is 'not uncommon' for young people to become involved in prostitution to support their own or others' drug habits (O'Neill *et al.*,1995).

Although this is a small sample, it is worrying that for those under 25 this appeared to be a motivation for entry into prostitution more frequently than it was for those over 25. Seven of the younger group were using drugs before they became involved in prostitution and half (13) started using them after getting involved in prostitution. This contrasts with only two of the over-25s using drugs prior to entering prostitution, though six started using them later on. Generally, then, there are different patterns in the way in which drug-taking is related to prostitution.

Nicki, who was 14 at the time of the interview, had become involved in prostitution the previous year. She had first been looked after when she was five after her mother had left her and her younger siblings with their violent, alcoholic and drug addicted father. Nicki was then adopted when she was ten and in the process had been separated from two of her siblings. A year after she was adopted Nicki's natural father died from a drugs overdose after which she started 'being naughty'. She was returned to care by her adoptive parents and became involved in prostitution when she ran away with a friend. She said,

I thought it were good at first but then I didn't want to go down there again [to the beat]. But I had to for drugs.

Nicki said she was using cannabis and had tried 'phet' (amphetamine) and heroin. According to the project worker who introduced us, Nicki also took heroin but the other working women with whom she is in contact try to dissuade her from using it.

Of the other seven participants who did not cite money as their primary reason for entering prostitution, five said they had been forced into prostitution by 'boyfriends'/pimps while two explicitly linked their entry into prostitution with the experience of sexual abuse. One linked it with being raped by her father when she was 12, and one cited being 'interfered with by various men' from the age of nine.

CHOOSING PROSTITUTION

Although money, drugs or coercion were the primary motivating factors for young people becoming involved in prostitution, other considerations often informed the decision to take this particular path. Given that many were too young to work legally in the formal labour market and many had not or could not consider begging because they considered it too degrading, prostitution was viewed as a more attractive alternative than other illegal options, essentially because they were aware that they could not be sent to prison for it. This highlights some of the anomalies which pervade the current debate on the legal status of prostitution.

Neil was 13 when he first became involved in prostitution and said he did so because he wanted money for drugs. He was 20 at the time of the interview and said,

It was my way of being safe and not getting myself locked up.

Dawn, who also wanted money for drugs, said,

I did it really cos of me heroin addiction, you know, to feed that, instead of going out shoplifting and burglaring, cos like I've been to prison as well, I just got out of prison two month ago, and when I came out of prison I thought, 'I'm not going back to prison, I'll just stick to working like I were doing before' cos I was doing alright... when I came out of prison I was clean. I did me rattle and that in jail. But out here it's dead easy, ye know, people are putting it [heroin] *in your face all the time. So instead of going out robbing, or mugging someone, or burglaring, I'll just work on corner, you know, with me friend.*

Dawn was still involved in prostitution at the time of the interview and had started using heroin again but said she only did so now if she was bored.

Chloe, who was 20 at the time of the interview and still involved in prostitution, had been using heroin for five and a half years and had also been using 'crack' for the past three. She was sent to live with her grandmother when she was 15 because she didn't get on with her stepfather. She became looked after at 16 because she had been running away from home and truanting from school. She said she hated her grandmother for placing her in public care. She first became involved in prostitution when she was 16 because she had started using heroin and wanted money for drugs. She said that she had to get her money for drugs somehow and she was 'no good at shoplifting'. She did not want to get involved in shoplifting because it carried a greater risk of a prison sentence.

Anita, who was 37 at the time of the interview, was also a heroin addict and still involved in prostitution. She first became involved at 16. She had been in prison three times for burglary and fraud which she committed to provide the money for drugs when she was having a break from prostitution. After her last spell in prison she decided she would stick to prostitution to provide the money for her heroin addiction because, although she could be fined for it, she knew she could only be sent to prison if she failed to pay her fines.

Louise, who first became involved in prostitution when she was 11, was using her income to provide food for herself and younger siblings because their violent, alcoholic mother was spending all the household income on alcohol. She was 17 at the time of the interview and had not been involved in prostitution for a year. She told us,

I didn't like it but I knew it were the only way I could get money without going thieving.

Josie was 14 when she first became involved in prostitution and 17 at the time of the interview. Before becoming involved in prostitution she had been caught and convicted for stealing and had decided that not only was prostitution 'less risky' but also that it was 'easy money'.

These accounts provide important insights into the way in which individuals assess the potential risks associated with different lifestyle choices. It is important to stress, however, that this was not a free choice, in the sense that young people were severely constrained by the nature of past experiences and current circumstances, including poverty, the absence of supportive family relationships and a safe home in which to live.

POWER AND POWERLESSNESS

There is also some evidence to suggest that for some of the participants who had been disempowered by their experiences at home and/or in care, prostitution afforded them the chance to feel powerful: in relation to the punters who made them feel extra special because they were paying for them; in relation to other non-working peers who did not have their spending power or purchasing capacity; and/or in relation to the authorities from whom they were seeking to avoid detection. Many said this sense of power and/or being aware of the dangers involved in what they were doing gave them a 'buzz' (Pitts, 1997; McMullen, 1989)

Lesley, whose story is opposite, describes the sense of power she felt when she first became involved in prostitution 'after being someone in a home people shouted at',

> *There's a big thing with power and there's a buzz with it as well you know, people don't often tell you about that . . . A lot of it was about feeling quite powerful, feeling as though I was in control. It was like going from nothing to something. I was the one who could get the money. I was the one that said when to stop and when to go. I was the one who could go out and spend. That was a tremendous buzz. It was very, very, powerful.*

When she was asked if she felt powerful in relation to the 'punters' she said,

> *Yes because you knew they were coming for you. You could tell them when to stop and when to go. And they were giving you things. They had to buy you. They couldn't just have you. They bought you because you were special. It made you feel a bit like mmmm, you know? And that's a big feeling.*

For others the 'buzz' was more to do with the dangers involved in what they were doing. Louise, whose experiences were described earlier, also said she enjoyed the 'buzz' of not getting caught and of 'pulling the wool over people's eyes'.

Lesley
Age: 40
Age of entry to prostitution: 13

Lesley was an only child of mixed parentage. She never knew her father. He was an American serviceman who deserted her mother and returned to the US when he knew she was pregnant. Lesley was brought up by her mother and grandparents until she was 13. Lesley described herself as a bit of a loner when she was a child and she used to travel across the city on her own to and from school from the age of six. On one of her journeys she was befriended by an old man who used to take her to the park, fondle her and give her sixpence for sweets. She would meet this old man quite often on her way home from school but never told anyone about it.

Lesley's grandparents died when she was about 12 and her mother found it hard to cope on her own. Lesley told the interviewer she looked after her mother more than her mother looked after her. As a result of her mother's inability to cope Lesley was placed in the care of the local authority when she was 13 from which she frequently ran away. At first she would always run home to her mother's who would return her to care and then she started running away to friends she knew who were older than her and had their own place to live. Lesley said she could never figure out where they got their money from but they always seemed to have some. One day one of her friends told her it was time she started earning her own money. Lesley didn't understand what she meant but was instructed by her friend about what to do, how much to charge and how to go about the business of prostitution.

By the time she was 15 Lesley had her own place to live and was supporting herself with the income she made from prosititution. She found this a very empowering experience. At 16 she got married and then had three children but continued her involvement in prostitution. She tried to leave prostitution when her children were small and took a job as a cleaner. She found, however, that the money was not enough to keep her family and returned to prostitution. She did not consider that her husband was 'pimping' her and was quite happy to be the breadwinner while he took responsibility for the household. Lesley had exited from prostitution four years before the interview, primarily because of her concern that she might not be providing a good role model for her children. She had also divorced her husband who had custody of her children whom she sees regularly. Since leaving prostitution and her marriage Lesley has settled happily into a lesbian relationship and has a good job.

How?

When asked about how they became involved in prostitution, over half the sample (27) said this was through peer group associations while a quarter (13) said they had become involved on a freelance basis. A minority of just ten participants said they were coerced into prostitution by someone else and almost two-thirds of this group (six) were in the over-25 age group. Many of the participants in fact made a point of asserting their independence from 'pimps': they said things like, 'I've never worked for a pimp and I never will', or 'I've never worked for a man and I never will', or, 'I only work for myself'. It is also worthy of note that of the ten who said they were forced into prostitution at least two were coerced by women rather than by men.

The fact that many of the women in this sample became involved in prostitution apparently without the coercion of a pimp contradicts other evidence which suggests that 'between 80 per cent and 95 per cent of prostitution is pimp controlled' (Faugier and Sergeant, 1997) and that the coercion and manipulation of young women by older men is the most common method by which young women become involved in prostitution (Swann, 1998). It has, however, been asserted by Armstrong (1993) that 'pimps play a minor role' in the recruitment of women into prostitution.

While approximately equal proportions (a quarter) of each age group said they entered prostitution on a freelance basis, those who were under 25 at the time of the interview said much more frequently than those over 25 that they became involved through friends they knew. Almost two-thirds (16) of the younger age group gave this reply compared to under half (11) of the older age group.

Nicki first became involved when she ran away from care with a friend through whom she met another friend who was already 'working'. She told us,

> she were one [a prostitute] *and she said it were easy money. So I decided to go on* ['the game'] . . . *Me friends got me into it and I just enjoyed it.*

Kate had run away from home with a friend. She said she met a 'lass'

> *and she were right nice to me all the time. I looked up to her when I were younger. An' she asked me to come to her uncle's and when I got there it were all 'take your clothes off'.*

After she had stripped, the 'uncle' asked her to perform oral sex and then paid her for it.

Kim was 17 at the time of the interview. She had just had a baby in the previous month. She had been placed in care at the age of 11 because she had been running away from home to escape her father's violence – which she was too scared to tell anyone about. While she was in care she made friends with another girl who was already 'working'. The friend took Kim with her to 'the beat' and she 'ended up doing a punter'.

Lisa said,

> *I've grown up around it so I know about it. Cos I live round the area I know people. I know like loads of 'em. I used to yap to them an' then one day it just happened. And I've done it ever since.*

We have already heard from Lesley, above, who told us she became involved through friends she was running to when she was running away from care. She felt she was running away to 'people who understood you' and who 'made you feel like a person'. When her friend told her it was now time she started earning her own living, Lesley replied,

'What do you mean?' and she said, 'Well this is a pack of durex. I'll show you where to go' which was at that time down this street here [indicating]. *And there used to be some cafes down the road there and we went outside and she said, 'You nod and tell the man'. When I first started I was thirteen. It was £2 in the car.*

Rachel said,

I did actually start working when I was 14, but that were one of me boyfriends that got me into that an' all, cos he had a habit and I had a small habit. An' I just thought I didn't care anyway.

Jenny entered prostitution on a 'freelance' basis, that is, she made the decision to become a prostitute on her own, albeit under some pressure created by the considerable sum of money she was offered (see p. 28). However, she also indicates the importance of peer groups and pre-existing associations and acquaintances within the world of prostitution. Before she became involved in prostitution herself she was friendly with other prostitutes and although she used to 'hang around and talk to them' she never thought she would 'do it' herself.

The principal mechanisms through which participants became involved in prostitution are summarised in Table 3.

Table 3 *How participants became involved in prostitution (n=50)*

Involved through peer groups	27
Freelance	13
Coerced by another into prostitution	10

The evidence suggests that the significance of peer group influence on a young person's decision to become involved in prostitution should not be underestimated and indeed that such influences are important in young people's entry into prostitution has been noted in recent research (Farmer and Pollock, 1998; O'Neill *et al.*, 1995). Consequently, the findings from this study suggest that attention should also be given to the importance of peer groups as well as to direct forms of coercion (or 'pimping'), which appeared less important for the participants in this study. It may be that this is indicative of a changing cultural context, and that peer groups and friendship networks seem to be more important in influencing the decision to enter prostitution for young people in the 1980s and 1990s than they were in the 1950s or 1960s. The significance of peer groups in initiating girls and young women into drug use has been noted in recent research (Maher, 1995). Research is also drawing attention to bullying and abusive relationships between young people, both in schools and in residential institutions such as children's homes, and these may also be important in understanding the peer group influence.

The significance of peer groups as a route into prostitution which has been found in this study suggests that the model of the 'prostitution triangle' (Swann, 1998) does not capture the complexity of what is actually going on. It suggests that a model of 'drift' (Davis 1978; Jesson, 1993; Crosby, 1997; Crosby and Barrett, 1999) is more appropriate than a model of coercion (Swann, 1998) to understanding the experience. Young people seem to be indirectly pushed, by the circumstances of their lives, into prostitution more than they are directly coerced by another person.

It seems that for many young people in contemporary society, the context of their lives is such that rather than an absence of 'relationships and networks that might prevent their drift into self-destructive and self-defeating behaviour' (Pitts, 1997), the networks and relationships in which they are embedded actually facilitate or encourage such self-destructive behaviour.

The evidence that many young people adopt prostitution as a survival strategy when they are on the run or appear to 'choose' it as a means of income generation which is preferable to other illegal and/or informal options should, however, be treated with a little caution. It is important to bear in mind evidence from other research with young homeless people which has suggested that vulnerable young people may consciously or unconsciously exaggerate, or 'creatively reinterpret' events so as to emphasise their degree of control over them (Hutson and Liddiard, 1994; Shaw and Butler, 1998). It is also important to bear in mind Marx's observation that 'we make our own histories but not in circumstances that we freely choose' (Kamenka, 1983). This is not to deny the 'agency' or self-determination of young people involved in prostitution (Scambler and Scambler, 1997) but to recognise that such choices are 'powerfully determined by negative experiences and reduced circumstances which constrain young people to act in ways which are inimical to their best interests' (Pitts, 1997). When their 'choice' is viewed in this way it becomes easier to understand why prostitution appears to be a viable option for some young people.

SUMMARY

- The majority of young people interviewed were motivated to enter prostitution by economic need. For some it was a survival strategy in the context of running away while others saw it as a means of achieving a material standard of living which they could not otherwise provide for themselves. The majority entered prostitution before they were legally old enough to enter the formal labour market.

- The majority became involved through peer associations and the role of coercion seemed to be less important than has previously been suggested by other research. Indeed, many young people seemed to 'drift' into prostitution.

- Over two-thirds of the sample became involved in prostitution before they could legally consent to sex.

4

How do young people experience prostitution?

This chapter deals with some of the experiences young people related to us about their involvement in prostitution. It will explore the nature of their involvement in prostitution; their responses to their first experiences of involvement; their experience of violence; their attitudes to the law and decriminalisation; the difficulties they encountered as a result of the legal status of prostitution; and what they thought about men who pay for sex with young girls and boys.

Their experiences of involvement in prostitution are summarised in Table 4 below.

Table 4 *Participants' experiences in prostitution (n=50)*

Continuous involvement since first time	25
Full-time involvement	32
Still involved at time of interview	33
Experience of violence/assault	24
Using/had used drugs	28

NATURE OF INVOLVEMENT IN PROSTITUTION

Half the sample (25) had been continuously involved in prostitution since they had first become involved. Amongst the other half, people had occasionally taken breaks, sometimes for a couple of months, sometimes to take up formal employment and sometimes as a result of having been in prison. Prostitution is not, therefore, necessarily a permanent occupation. Lisa explained her involvement thus:

It was just on and off, on and off. Say like when I was stuck for money or whatever. And say like working at the care assistant job,

cos I got paid there monthly coming towards the end of the
month, the last week or so, I'd be skint so I used to go out there a
lot. At one point I was doing it all the time. Then I stopped again
for about six months. Then I'd start again. It's not all the time.

Approximately two-thirds of participants said they were involved in prostitution on a full-time basis – that is they would work every day and in a couple of instances every day and every night. Almost three-quarters of the sample (36) described themselves as 'street workers', that is they worked 'on the beat' instead of from houses or flats. A small group had combined working on the street with working from houses or flats and just a few had worked solely from houses or premises such as houses, flats, saunas and massage parlours. This may of course be due to the particular nature and location of the projects through which participants were accessed.

FIRST EXPERIENCES IN PROSTITUTION

One thing all the participants had in common, regardless of how long they had been involved in prostitution or how long ago they had exited, was that they could all remember their first experience of prostitution. For many it had been a fairly traumatic event. Kate said she was 'scared' and 'embarrassed' on the first occasion, but afterwards decided that it was 'easy money'. Josie said,

It made me feel miles away for days. It made me feel right out of
it for days. Not me . . . and then I did another one and another and
it just . . . it got easier.

Others spoke of feeling dirty and/or feeling that 'it weren't right' or of feeling ashamed. Dawn said she felt 'really dirty' after her first time but she was more concerned about getting some money so that she wouldn't 'get beaten up' by her boyfriend.

VIOLENCE

Earlier chapters have highlighted the violence which a high proportion of interviewees had experienced within their families. Many continued to be the victims of violence after entering prostitution. Although in the total sample only ten people said they became involved in prostitution because they were forced or 'pimped', several of the women (but none of the men) had become mixed up with pimps and/or were in relationships with violent men after they became involved. In some cases the women were forced to work by these violent partners who were taking their money off them but in other instances the violent partner seemed to be unaware of the source of the woman's income.

Almost half the sample, 24 in all, reported that they had experienced violence at the hands of partners, pimps or punters. Evidence from other research has also suggested that violence is quite central to the experience of those on the street (Dean and Melrose, 1999) and to those involved in prostitution in particular (O'Neill, 1994). For some it took much longer to get away from the pimp/partner than it did for others. This is also the case in evidence presented by Faugier and Sergeant (1997). It seemed to be especially difficult for the women to break away when the relationship was one of pimp-as-partner or partner-as-pimp.

We have heard above, for example, that Dawn became involved in a relationship and had a baby at 15. She and the baby went to live with the boyfriend when she was 16. The boyfriend, who was using heroin, initiated her into heroin and they both developed habits. The boyfriend became extremely violent to both Dawn and the baby when he didn't have any heroin. Dawn saw the solution to this as 'working' to supply the money. She was adamant that he thought she had a job in a bar and did not know how she was really getting the money and that she made the decision to go 'on the beat' on her own. She managed to escape from the boyfriend and get out of the relationship when he went to prison. Although she has moved to another city she remains scared of the boyfriend but doesn't think he will find her.

DRUGS

Other research evidence has found high rates of drug use amongst people working in prostitution (Blom and van den Berg, 1989; McKeganey *et al.*, 1990; Faugier *et al.*, 1992; Crosby, 1997; Plant, 1997; Crosby and Barrett, 1999; Curren and Sinclair, 1998) and that young women often become involved in prostitution to provide for their own and/or their partner's drug habits (O'Neill *et al.*, 1995). The participants in this sample were no exception. In all just over half the participants (28) were, or had been, using drugs such as heroin, crack and/or amphetamine. There were regional variations in the types of drugs that were used most prevalently.

As has been noted above, those who said they were or had been using drugs were most often in the under-25 age group. Of those who were using or had been using drugs, approximately a third (nine) were using them before they became involved in prostitution and over three-quarters (seven) of this group were under 25. The rest of those who were or had been using drugs (19) began using them after entry into prostitution. Many acknowledged that they were stuck in a circle of needing drugs to cope with the work and then needing to work because they couldn't function properly without the drugs. This has also been found in other research studies (Curren and Sinclair, 1998).

Kate said she sometimes felt, 'I can't be bothered going out tonight, I'll just stay in and watch the telly. But I can't because of heroin'. We also heard earlier from Nicki who said that even though she didn't want to go onto 'the beat' again she 'had to for drugs'.

The prevalence of drug use amongst the younger age group should be understood in the context of a general increase in drug use, particularly heroin, amongst young unemployed people throughout the 1980s (Dorn and South, 1987). For example, in 1992 the Institute for Drug Dependence found that whereas one in 20 adults had used illicit drugs, the figure for the under-25 age group was one in 8. In 1990, 32 per cent (5800) of all Home Office notified drug addicts were under 25 and in the same year 45 per cent of all new addicts notified to the Home Office were under 25 (British Youth Council, 1992). The extent of drug use amongst the younger age group lends some support to the views of the Government's newly appointed 'drug tzar' that 'Britain is on the edge of a new teenage heroin epidemic' (Crosby and Barrett, 1999).

ATTITUDES TO THE LAW AND DECRIMINALISATION

As we saw in the Introduction (p. 4), many people now argue that child prostitution should be decriminalised, i.e. that people under 18 involved in prostitution should not be processed through the criminal justice system. When the participants were asked about this, they found it difficult conceptually to distinguish between decriminalisation and legalisation. Many of the people interviewed were not particularly troubled about the legal status of prostitution. Indeed, as was pointed out in Chapter 3, many of the participants regarded prostitution as the more attractive illegal option, primarily because they knew they could not go to prison for it. Many in fact saw fines as 'just part of the job' and one woman ingeniously suggested that the money taken in fines should be used directly to fund programmes for preventing young people from becoming involved in prostitution and for supporting those who are involved to get out of it.

Almost three-quarters (36) of the participants had been cautioned for prostitution. Just over two-thirds (18) of those who revealed the age at which they were first cautioned (26) were under 18 when they received it and of these just over half (ten) were under 16 when they received their first caution. A slightly smaller proportion of the sample, approximately half (24), had convictions for prostitution and a third (15) of those who gave their age at first conviction said they were under 18 when they were first convicted. As we might expect, there were more people with convictions aged over 25 at the time of the interview than under 25. Approximately two-thirds (15) of the older age group had convictions compared to just over a third of the younger age group (ten). However, worryingly, almost a third (four) of those who were 18 and under at the time of the interview had already been convicted for prostitution. None of the men had been cautioned or convicted.

Table 5 summarises participants' experiences of the law and their views about it.

Table 5 *Participants' experiences of and views on the law (n=50)*

Nos with cautions	36
Cautioned before 18	18
Cautioned before 16	10
Nos with convictions	24
Convicted before 18	15
Legal status complicates life	24
Think more young people involved compared to when young	38

On the other hand, nearly half the sample (24), whether they had convictions or not, thought that the legal status of prostitution made their lives more difficult and there were a number of ways in which this happened. While many accepted the 'work–fine–work' cycle, others talked about the stupidity and futility of this and argued that when they were fined they were left with no alternative but to return to prostitution.

Jenny found being arrested irritating because 'it makes us go back out because we haven't made anything'. She found it difficult to understand why she should be arrested: 'Why can't the police just leave us alone? It's our bodies. I just don't understand why they just don't leave us alone'. Helen, who was 17 at the time of the interview and 13 when she first became involved in prostitution, thought, 'The police should leave us to do what we're doing and get off our case basically'. A quarter of participants thought that the legal status of prostitution had made no difference to their lives. Many of these said whether it was legal or illegal if you needed to do it you would.

Some of the women thought that the role of the police was simply to 'harass' them and didn't like having to 'worry about the cops and getting picked up on the street'. This worry made them feel they had to keep moving around and 'ducking and diving' to avoid detection by the authorities. In this respect the mobility of a small group of the participants was quite remarkable; some had 'worked' in a number of major towns and cities both in Britain and further afield. These women said that if they were cautioned in one area they would simply move somewhere else, and would use false names so that they were never cautioned twice in the same area using the same name. One woman had used over 20 different names at one point in her life. It is also worthy of note that some of the women told us that they had actually had experienced less 'hassle' from the police when they were working as juveniles than they had since they had been working as adults. More than one told us that 'no-one bothered with us' when they were juveniles.

Many participants told us that they felt unable to go to the police if they were assaulted, raped or the victim of other crime. They felt that if they were to report crimes committed against them they would not be taken seriously. Comments such as 'once they know you're a working girl they don't want to know' were not uncommon. One woman who

had been viciously raped by her ex-husband during the six months pre-
ceding the interview had not bothered to report it because her friend

*had a similar experience – being raped, like, and when she went
to the police, once they knew she was a working girl it was awful.
I didn't want to go through all that. It wasn't worth it.*

Evidence from the English of Collective of Prostitutes (Adams *et
al.*, 1997; ECP, 1997) has also shown that the law does not afford
'working women' the same civil rights as other citizens and evidence
from a study of people involved in begging has shown that they feel
similarly about not being able to report crimes committed against them
(Dean and Melrose, 1999).

For Chloe the feeling that she would not be taken seriously because
she was a 'smack head and a prostitute' extended to other professionals
beyond the police. At the time of the interview Chloe's foot was very
badly swollen. When she was asked what she had done she said she
had fallen down some stairs a couple of weeks before but she had also
been 'shooting up in it'. She said she had not seen a doctor because
'once they know you're a smack head and a prostitute they don't want
to know'.

Despite the fact that many said the legal status of prostitution made
their lives more difficult only a minority of participants (seven) were
in favour of decriminalising prostitution for *everyone*. This was true
for similar proportions of both the under and over-25s.

Responses to the question of whether interviewees supported the
decriminalisation of prostitution for people under 18 revealed interest-
ing age differences. Those in the under-25 age group were much more
in favour of the decriminalisation of prostitution for those who were
over 18, while, probably unsurprisingly, only three of the over-25s
expressed this view. In regard to decriminalisation for the under-18s,
most of the over-25s – two-thirds – said simply 'no' in response to the
question.

Those who were not in favour of decriminalisation for those under
18 gave a number of reasons for this but the general consensus was
that young people should not 'need to be there anyway'. Some participants thought that decriminalisation might make prostitution more
attractive, because 'there'd be no hiding away; they'd just go down
there and do it'. Some worried that if it were decriminalised more

young people would become involved and many said that it was not something they would want for their daughters. Most participants thought that young people should be helped and supported to get out of prostitution or prevented from becoming involved in the first place.

Zoe was 24 and no longer involved in prostitution at the time of the interview. She had become involved at 16, but had made the decision to change her way of life when she was 20 after her son had died a cot death. When she was asked if she thought more young people would become involved if it were decriminalised she said, 'I don't know really... It's not an occupation you want to go into. It's just something you fall into I think'. She was not in favour of decriminalisation and thought young women should be helped to exit from the lifestyle.

Chloe thought it should be legalised for women over 19. She felt that young girls who become involved are 'naive' and would only be encouraged by decriminalisation. Others like Kate, who had first become involved at 12, objected to decriminalisation on the grounds that, 'At 12, 13, 14 you shouldn't be doing it [having sex] anyway'. Nicki, who first became involved at 13 objected to decriminalisation on the grounds that girls under 16 were 'not ready' for sex: 'Your body's not ready for it'.

For a couple of participants the fact that it was illegal made it more 'fun'. Louise, who became involved at 11, thought 'because it wasn't legal it was more fun... It was probably more fun than it actually being legalised'. Lesley was also attracted by the illegality. She said,

> I think probably if it had not been illegal I wouldn't have done it. Well, no, I mean, the whole point about it then was, it was about making money cos I didn't have any other way, but I mean if it had not been illegal probably other people wouldn't have been doing it or there would have been structures in place telling you 'this is harder than you think'.

Despite their views on decriminalisation for those under 18, over three-quarters (38) of participants did think that more young people were involved in prostitution today compared with when they started. Many of these thought that more young people were becoming involved because they were addicted to drugs.

Lawrence, who was 18 at the time of the interview and had a history of running away from both home and care, had become involved in prostitution when he was 13 and 'on the run'. He felt that more young boys were involved 'because it's so hard to get money these days'. Richard, who became involved at 14 and was 25 at the time of the interview, also thought that more young people were involved than when he first became involved himself. He also thought they were motivated primarily by money. Richard had no history of care and no history of running away from home. He had become involved in prostitution because he 'wanted the experience' and found that being paid was 'an added bonus'. That Richard became involved because he wanted the sexual experience bears out the perceptions of practitioners in the field who think that boys become involved in 'renting' because they are not old enough legitimately to gain access to the gay scene (McNeish, 1998). However, he was the only male interviewed to cite this as a reason.

EARNINGS AND AGE

Many of the participants were also aware that 'the younger you are the more you earn'. Neil had noticed that his own income had declined as he had got older. He said, 'As you get older you seem to get less and less' and said that when he was 13, 14, 15 he had earned more than he had since he was 16.

Dawn spoke quite matter-of-factly about 'young girls' always being able 'to make a lot of money because punters like fresh meat and they go for a new face'. For her this was an incentive to move between areas to work. Zoe said, 'When you're a new face you get more customers anyway'. When she was asked if she thought more young girls were involved now than when she started she said, 'From what I can tell, yeah, cos the money's in... the younger you are the more you earn'. Lesley also acknowledged that younger women tended to earn more money and also thought that many more young women were now involved compared with when she had become involved herself.

These views on decriminalisation and the involvement of young girls in prostitution should perhaps be understood within the context of the highly competitive market in which they operate. In view of what they say about the earning potential of young girls, there may be an element of self-interest informing their views on decriminalisation.

VIEWS ON PENALTIES FOR MEN USING YOUNG PEOPLE

If they were not in favour of decriminalising prostitution for those under 18, many of the participants were in favour of introducing severe penalties for the people who use under-age prostitutes. When asked what they thought should be done about these men, suggestions of castration were not uncommon. Josie thought they should 'get their knobs knocked off' because 'they can cause little girls damage'. Lorraine thought they 'need their heads kicking in' and Louise thought 'they want shooting, they are perverts'. Kerry, a 22-year-old (trans-sexual), had become involved in prostitution at 17 because she was 'sick of being chased by men' and thought she 'might as well get paid for it', suggested 'lambing shears' when she was asked what she thought should be done about men who pay for sex with young people. Others suggested they should be 'hung' or 'locked up and throw away the key'.

Some were a little kinder in their attitudes and thought these men 'needed help'. Others talked about the difficulties for men in knowing a girl's real age because they 'often lie' about it and dress to make themselves look much older than they really are. Curiously, of those who were asked if they thought the men who had paid for them when they were under age were 'perverts' most said 'no'. Liz, who had become involved at 13 when she had run away from home, was 42 at the time of the interview and said she did not think of them as perverts because she had 'always had an old head on my shoulders'.

SUMMARY

- The findings from this study suggest that most of the women had become involved in prostitution on a full-time basis, many had taken breaks and only half had been continuously involved since their first entry.

- Violence from partners, punters and/or pimps was central to the experience for 24 of the sample.

- Drug use was relatively high amongst the whole group but particularly high amongst the under-25 age group.

- The majority were not in favour of decriminalisation for those under 18 but many were in favour of severe penalties for the men who pay for sex with young people.

- A majority had been cautioned for prostitution and of these most were cautioned before they were 18. A smaller proportion had been convicted for prostitution although it is clear that many were still being criminalised for their activities. Many thought that the legal status of prostitution made their lives more difficult, but ironically some felt they had actually experienced less trouble from the police when they were children.

- The strategies which they adopted to avoid detection by the authorities, such as moving to different areas and/or assuming false identities, meant that they were a highly mobile and transient population. This has implications for the development and delivery of services for this group, including social work and child protection procedures, and also for official statistics which attempt to measure the scale of the problem from official records of numbers of cautions and convictions.

CHAPTER 5

What makes young people stay in prostitution?

A t the time of the interviews just over a third (18) of participants had exited from prostitution while 32 remained involved. Of those who were no longer involved some had exited from the lifestyle over five years previously while others had not 'worked' in the fortnight or month before the interview. Similar proportions of each age group were still involved in prostitution at the time of the interview: just over two-thirds (18) of the under-25 age group and just under two-thirds (14) of the over-25 group.

The focus of this study is child prostitution, and to include the views of older individuals on what makes young people stay in prostitution may therefore seem questionable. However, in addition to the fact that some of the older group were not so very far from their experiences as children, it was a striking feature of the interviews that most participants did not make a conceptual distinction between working as a prostitute as a child and working as an adult. Qualitatively, it seemed, there was little difference in the experiences involved.

MONEY AND WORK

As we saw in Chapter 3, the vast majority of participants became involved in prostitution before they were old enough to enter the formal labour market or to claim welfare benefits in their own right and, as we have seen, many did not feel they had any alternative means of generating the income they wanted. The things they told us when we asked about what it was that made it difficult for them to get out of prostitution indicated that labour market conditions and the inadequacy of welfare benefits in meeting their needs were important factors in keeping them in prostitution once they had become involved. Many of the young people we spoke to were aware of their restricted opportunities in the labour market and were conscious of the fact that all that was available for them were 'shit jobs and govvy schemes' (Coffield *et al.*, 1986). While these findings should be placed in the context of the family stress and other problems that most of this group had experienced, it seemed that their willingness to participate in the formal labour market had been undermined by low pay and the insecure or temporary nature of the employment available to them (Wilkinson, 1994).

Almost half the sample (22) said it was lack of money which prevented them from getting out of prostitution but once again there were marked differences by age groups. Half (13) of the under-25 age group said it was lack of money which prevented their exit compared to just over a third (nine) of the over-25 group.

Dawn, who was 24 at the time of the interview, was clear that the formal labour market could not provide her with the opportunities to make the sort of income she made from prostitution. She asked us,

What job pays £60, £100 a night? Sometimes you can earn £100 in an hour if it's busy. You know where you're well off, don't you?

Dawn did not see herself getting out of prostitution in the future. She told us,

I like it. I don't like the sex part of it, I just like the money part of it.

Carol, who became involved in prostitution when she was 13 and living at home with her mother, was 37 at the time of the interview. She lived with her partner and her two young sons. In her view 'money is power' and she said she was not prepared to work for £80 per week in the formal labour market because she would not be able to pay her household bills. She said the only thing that would make her consider getting out of prostitution was 'winning the lottery' but even then she thought she might still see her 'regulars'.

Zoe, who as we have seen had exited from prostitution, talked about how the need for money continually tempted her to return to it. She found it was difficult to remain friends with the people she used to know because of the 'temptation' involved in seeing 'all the money they've got when you've got nothing'.

Susan told us, 'Money, money, money's still the reason why I'm doing it'. Josie told us, 'It's money all the time'. Tina, who first became involved in prostitution through a friend when she was 15, was

23 but no longer involved at the time of the interview. She said it was 'money and the security of money' which had kept her involved. Kim, who as we saw earlier first became involved at 11, was 17 and still involved at the time of the interview. She did not see herself getting out of prostitution. She said she 'needed the money' and now that she had a child to support she needed the money even more.

Karen was no longer involved in prostitution at the time of the interview. She was 18 when interviewed and had first become involved when she was 14. She said what had made it difficult for her to get out was 'the fact that I could get easy money. It was just easy money'. She was aware that she had no alternative means of achieving the same level of income from formal employment or from any other source and spoke about the 'feelgood factor' involved in going home at the end of a night with '£200 in your pocket'.

Sally was 24 at the time of the interview and had become involved in prostitution when she was 15. She also felt that there was 'no way she could earn the money from anything else'.

Alison was 30 at the time of the interview and had become involved in prostitution when she was 17 when she and a friend went out for the evening and she was approached and offered £25 by a 'punter'. At the time of the interview she lived with her partner and two children. She had tried to get out of prostitution a few times in the past but she said, 'The kids keep bringing me out of retirement. There are lots of outgoings, school trips and holidays and things'.

Sandra had become involved in prostitution when she was 13 and had run away from care which she had entered because she had 'got mixed up with the wrong crowd' and because she didn't get on with her stepmother. She was 38 at the time of the interview and still involved. She had also tried to exit in the past and had worked as a care assistant for which she earned just £3.40 an hour and found that she needed to supplement her income from the formal labour market with income from prostitution. She gave up the job eventually and returned to prostitution on a full-time basis.

We heard earlier from Lisa who also used prostitution as a means of supplementing income from the formal economy. She had worked as a care assistant but had now given up that job and was working in a chip shop and supplementing her income through prostitution. She doesn't 'work' (in prostitution) everyday 'but whenever I need the money'.

Marie was 24 at the time of the interview and, apart from an eight-month break when she got a 'proper job', had been involved in prostitution since she was 15. Marie had become fed up with her mother who 'went out drinking a lot', leaving Marie to look after her younger siblings. At 15 Marie's grandmother had arranged for her to go and live with her cousin, with whom she became involved in prostitution. She was still involved at the time of the interview and did not see herself exiting from the lifestyle in the foreseeable future. She had tried to get out of prostitution in the past and had taken a job in a factory for eight months. However, she was only earning £15 a day and couldn't survive on the money. She said she kept comparing her earnings from the factory to what she could make in prostitution. The amounts of money and the time required to make it in her factory job bore no comparison to prostitution so she gave up the job and returned to prostitution full time.

Some participants, like Rose, who had become involved in prostitution when she was 17 and was 40 and still involved at the time of the interview, thought that she 'couldn't do a proper job now'. Kate, 18 at the time of interview, agreed, on the grounds that she could not do a proper job now because of her heroin habit (see pp. 17–18).

When Lesley, who was no longer involved in prostitution at the time of the interview, was asked what had kept her involved for so long she said, '(a) The money; (b) then it became a habit and (c) then there were the kids'. She said that, 'Prostitution is a bit like smoking cigarettes. You go straight back to it when times get tough'. Lesley also felt that it was difficult to leave because all her friends were involved in prostitution and she thought, 'The longer you are involved the more difficult it becomes to get a real job in the real world'. Her full story is given on pp. 33–4.

Pauline had grown up in a children's home, and became involved in prostitution when she was 15 and on the run from care. She was 48 at the time of the interview but had not been involved in prostitution for the past eight years. However, when she was asked what had prevented her from getting out before then, she said it was lack of money: 'You get used to the money and know that you can't make that kind of money doing anything else'. She said prostitution 'messes you up mentally' and stressed that it 'looks like easy money but it really isn't'.

Nicki, aged 14 at interview, said she had 'quit' prostitution at the time of the interview primarily because she didn't like doing it. She said she had become involved and stayed involved for seven months because she had no money. Nicki's account if anything emphasised her immaturity: she talked about her friend who 'gets loads' of pocket money from her parents: 'She gets a fiver every day and £10 at weekends. I wish I got that.' Although she didn't like being involved in prostitution because 'I think it's dirty and I just don't like doing it. It's easy money but...', she recognised that if she needed money she would probably go back to it: 'But if I need some money I'll probably end up going back on game'.

As well as being aware that they had nothing like the same earning potential in the formal labour market, some participants were also aware that they could not live on welfare benefits. Jenny told us 'social security couldn't keep me now'. She didn't think she would be able to get out of prostitution, 'I don't think I could leave that lifestyle now cos it's too easy'.

Josie, who we have heard from above, was 17 and still involved in prostitution at the time of the interview. She said she could not live on the £28 per week job seeker's allowance she received and when she is 'skint' she goes to 'work'. On some occasions, however, she said she chooses 'to ignore that I'm skint'.

Susan told us, 'I get benefits but it's never enough, is it?' She felt that, 'No matter how much you get on benefits it's not going to last you two weeks'.

Although two of the young men in the sample were no longer involved in prostitution at the time of the interview they too had found that it was lack of money which had kept them involved.

Pete was 26 at the time of the interview. He had adopted prostitution as a survival strategy after his father threw him out of home at 14 because he revealed that he was gay. He had been diagnosed HIV positive and was no longer involved in prostitution at the time of the interview. However, he said he had remained in prostitution until the time he was diagnosed because of his need for money, food and shelter.

Lawrence, who was 18 and still involved in 'renting' at the time of the interview, told us he remained in prostitution because he needed the money and did not have the qualifications to get a well paid job in the formal labour market. For him, prostitution was 'a quick, fast and easy way' of getting the money he needed.

Richard, who was 25 at the time of the interview, was still involved in prostitution, because, he said, he knew that he could not earn what he made from renting in a proper job.

The reasons why individuals enter and remain in prostitution are complex and should not be reduced to any single factor. However, the testimonies of these young people indicate that social and labour market policies are a factor in their entrapment in prostitution. This reiterates the point made in Chapter 1, namely that the economic and political context of recent years has not, on the whole, acted to prevent young people from using prostitution as a means to circumvent the constraints of their circumstances. Since the 1980s, unemployment and/or low pay has been a central feature of young people's lives. In 1992, 16- and 17-year-old males who were working full time received just one third of the wages paid to full-time (adult) male workers (Dean, 1997). Throughout the 1980s, the unemployment rate for those aged between 16 and 19 stood at 20 per cent (France, 1996). In the first nine months of 1992, the number of young people who were unemployed and without an income (as a result of changes to their entitlement to benefits) rose from 70,000 to 97,000 (Dean, 1997). By 1994, over three-quarters of 16- and 17-year-olds who were registered as unemployed were without any income (France, 1996). Those who are in receipt of benefits have found that their value has declined considerably as a proportion of average earnings (Oppenheim and Lister, 1996). It is not therefore surprising that many young people resort to informal income generating strategies such as prostitution and begging in order to survive.

Additionally, many of the young people who revealed what they had earned per week from prostitution cited figures that were often approximating £1000 per week (and more in some cases). Many said that they aimed for earnings in the region of £100 per night, although some admitted that this wasn't always possible. However, given these incomes it is not difficult to see why prostitution should appear to many participants to be a route to 'easy money'. Even had they managed to obtain the well-paid jobs to which at least some aspired, it is unlikely that they would have access to such earnings. That said, when asked about the kind of income they thought they might need in order to get out of prostitution some of the participants mentioned surprisingly small sums.

Susan, for example, thought she would need 'a hundred pounds a week. It's not a lot but I would be able to survive. I mean that's all I want, I don't want to be rich, I don't want to be posh, I don't want to be high class. I just want to survive, that's all I want to do'.

Carol said she would need to 'clear' £150 per week from formal employment to consider getting out of prostitution, and Lawrence thought that if he could get a job which gave him £150 per week to live on he would be 'chuffed'. Marie, who said she had no plans to leave prostitution, said if she had a job which could provide £300 per week minimum she would consider getting out of prostitution.

It was also evident that many young people who were interviewed for the research were still attached to the work ethic. As we have seen earlier, the majority preferred the term 'working' to describe what they do. This was therefore a non-pejorative term which was important to the self-identity of the individuals concerned. It could also, however, act as a distancing device through which these women and men disassociate themselves from the stigma of prostitution (Shaw and Butler, 1998). Others talked of working for themselves, of being their own boss and of earning their living. Zoe told us that she couldn't work 'the hours I want and make the money I want' through any other job. She said she would never consider begging as an alternative to prostitution because people who beg are 'just waiting for people to give you money but not earning it. At least you're still earning your own money when you're working, even though you're earning it in a different way to most people'. These sentiments were echoed by a lot of the participants.

Despite the inability of some participants to see a way out of prostitution and their awareness that it provided them with better income-generating opportunities than the formal labour market, many did in fact, as we have seen, have aspirations to get out of prostitution. Their desire for 'normal' lifestyles was expressed in terms of wanting a 'decent job' and/or in terms of wanting to settle down, usually in a heterosexual relationship and have children. Despite the fact that their hopes and aspirations may be conditioned by early trauma, the evidence suggests that many do in fact share, with the majority of the population, aspirations to conventional lifestyles. This has also been found amongst those who are unemployed, those who 'fiddle' their welfare benefits and those who beg (Dean and Taylor-Gooby, 1992; Dean and Melrose, 1996, 1999).

Other participants clearly saw no way out of prostitution and had no plans to exit. They felt it was just 'too easy' to earn their money as they did. Two members of the sample, both in the under-25 age group, had aspirations for 'promotion' within the world of prostitution. One hoped she would be able to move away from street work and get a job in a sauna or massage parlour; the other said she would like to start her own 'red light business' in a town where there wasn't one already. Clearly for these two participants their willingness to enter the formal labour market, under any conditions, had been undermined by their experiences in prostitution.

DRUGS

As we have seen in previous chapters, the prevalence of drug use was much higher amongst the younger age group and approximately a quarter (six) of those under 25 said their need for drugs prevented them from getting out of prostitution compared to just one person in the over-25 age group.

Chloe, who was introduced earlier, said she was addicted to heroin and also using 'crack'. When she was asked about what prevented her from getting out of prostitution she said it was 'drugs and needing money for drugs'. She could see quite clearly the vicious circle she was trapped in. She said, 'I have to get off drugs to get off the beat and I need to get off the beat to get off drugs'.

Kate was also introduced earlier. She was pregnant at the time of the interview and addicted to heroin. She said it was her addiction which prevented her from getting out of prostitution and when asked if she would continue to work through the pregnancy she replied, 'I ain't got much choice, have I? It's either that or be sick'. She then went on to explain that if she didn't have heroin the unborn baby would also get sick and she would risk a miscarriage. As we heard earlier, Kate sometimes felt that she didn't want to go 'to the beat' but she had to 'because of heroin'. Kate's full story is given on pp. 17–18.

We also heard earlier from Nicki, aged 14, who also felt that she didn't want to go 'on the beat' again, 'but I had to for drugs'.

Naomi was 18 at the time of the interview and 15 when she first became involved in prostitution to support her and her boyfriend's heroin addiction. She said she couldn't earn the same money that she made from prostitution elsewhere and that she couldn't support her drug habit any other way. She said when she could get drugs without 'working' she had a break from prostitution. For example, she had lived with a drug dealer for a while and took a break from prostitution because he was supplying her with the drugs she needed. However, that relationship had since ended and she had no choice but to return to prostitution. Naomi's full story is given below.

Naomi
Age: 18
Age of entry to prostitution: 15

Naomi had a fairly 'normal', happy and stable home life until she was about 12. At this time she was told that she was in fact adopted and that the person she had always known as her uncle was actually her father. Her adoptive parents were actually her uncle and aunt. Naomi was greatly distressed by this information and started misbehaving – truanting from school, smoking heroin and getting into trouble. Her adoptive parents felt they couldn't cope with her behaviour any longer and when she was 15 sent her to live in a hostel. Shortly after this her adoptive mother died and Naomi started injecting heroin. She began working in prostitution at 15 to provide the money for her own and her boyfriend's drug habits.

At the time of the interview Naomi was still using heroin and still involved in prostitution. She was homeless and living in a hostel. She had never been given an opportunity to explore how she felt about finding out that she was adopted or about her adoptive mother dying. She felt that if there had been someone to talk to about these things she might never have started taking drugs and become involved in prostitution. Naomi had not been in touch with her family since her adoptive mother died; she felt she had hurt them too much for them to forgive her but she very much wanted to be able to re-establish contact. Naomi did not see herself getting out of prostitution in the forseeable future. She said it was primarily her need for money for drugs that kept her involved.

Valerie and Lorraine also said that they remained in prostitution because they had drug habits which they had to finance somehow.

When asked to say on a scale of one to ten how important they thought drugs were in keeping them involved in prostitution over three-quarters (19) of those who used them scored them at between six and ten. More alarming still, over three-quarters of those who were 18 and under at the time of the interview (ten) said that drugs were, to some extent, important in keeping them involved in prostitution and of these almost two-thirds (six) scored their importance at between six and ten. What is striking about these findings is the relative youthfulness of those who are already heavily involved in using highly addictive substances such as heroin and crack.

FRIENDSHIPS

Money and drugs, however, were not the only factors which made exit from prostitution difficult for the participants. Those in the over-25 age group tended to say that it was a combination of money and fear, either of the violent partners/pimps with whom they were in relationships or a fear of not having friends in the world beyond prostitution, which prevented them from getting out of it. This fear of having no friends was mentioned by a number of participants.

For Lesley and many of the other women the friendship networks which they formed while in prostitution acted as a form of surrogate family. Lesley told us that the group of people she 'hung around with' became her 'family' and that amongst these friends 'prostitution was the norm'. She talked of a 'community' of prostitutes which she said 'in its own way was quite caring'.

Liz was 42 and at the time of the interview was trying to exit from prostitution and had a job in a pub. However, she still saw her regular clients in order to top up her income from formal work. Liz also said that the group of friends she made while she was working became her family and it was difficult to get out because this also meant 'leaving all your friends'.

Pauline, who had successfully exited from prostitution at the time of the interview, also said that all her friends were 'working' and 'you feel alone when you leave them behind'.

Rachel, who was 18 at the time of the interview and had become involved in prostitution when she was 14 and living at home, said she had not been involved in prostitution for six months at the time of the interview. She had decided that 'there's more to life than working' but said it had been difficult for her to stop because she had no friends beyond the world of prostitution and that all her friends were 'bad people'.

Zoe, who had exited from prostitution four years ago, after the death of her son had made her decide she wanted to change her lifestyle, said, 'It's quite frightening once you're in there to try to get out because you've nobody to associate with at all'. She told us, 'When you're working the people you're working with become your family'.

Claire, who had become involved in prostitution when she was 14, was 39 at the time of the interview and was still involved. She had become involved in prostitution while missing from care. When asked what had kept her involved in prostitution she said it was lack of money and in addition to that she said 'you get trapped in the lifestyle' and that 'everyone within your circle of friends regards prostitution as normal'.

Other participants told us that as a result of their experiences in prostitution they felt it would be difficult for them to form relationships in the future. For example, Richard told us that he thought it would be difficult to have 'sex for pleasure' in the future and that it would be difficult to have a 'normal' relationship if he were to leave prostitution because his past would 'always be there'.

Many of the women spoke of difficulties in forming relationships because they were unable to trust men. Pauline, who was 48, had successfully exited from prostitution eight years before the interview after being involved for some 25 years. She was now in a relationship with a man who was 'the best bloke I've ever known'. However, she was finding the relationship difficult to sustain because of her inability to trust men; 'I can't help it', she said, 'I treat them all like punters. If I'm not getting anything from them they ain't getting anything from me'.

There was also a marked contrast between the ways in which older women and younger women in the sample described the relationships with other working women. As we have seen above, older women tended to talk of a 'family' of prostitutes and would talk about the way they used to 'watch out for each other'. The younger women, on the other hand, tended to describe situations which were much more competitive, violent and even predatory. Two young women from the north of England described a practice which they called 'taxing' whereby other women – often of the same age group – would take their money off them. This practice may fall within the realms of blackmail and is at least extortion. It was also described, and referred to in the same way, by people engaged in begging (Dean and Melrose, 1999). This practice of 'taxing' and of being beaten up by other women persuaded one young woman in this sample to get out of prostitution. Sadly, it represents another way in which young people entering prostitution can be preyed upon.

STIGMA

It was evident from what many of the participants said that getting out of prostitution was much more difficult than getting into it. Even those who had made the decision to exit from the lifestyle frequently felt tempted to return to prostitution either for economic or social reasons.

Bernadette, who had first became involved at 15 when she ran away from home, had left prostitution when she was 26. She was 30 at the time of the interview. Her decision to get out of prostitution was prompted by the murder of a friend which had made her lose her 'nerve'. She found she just could not get into a car after this incident and she felt that the 'punters' could sense her fear which made her more vulnerable. Bernadette talked about the difficulties of trying to re-build her life outside of prostitution. She said she was trying to get a job but had no CV and it was therefore very difficult for her to apply for jobs. She was living on income support at the time of the interview and had three children to provide for. She found that the money she received from social security wasn't enough and she was frequently tempted by the need for money to return to prostitution but her 'lack of nerve' prevented her from doing so. She also felt that it was difficult to 'shrug off' her past and is always fearful that she might bump into someone who knew her in her working life. Bernadette said she feels shunned by 'straight society'.

The awareness of the stigma that 'straight society' attaches to those who work in prostitution, rather than those who pay for their services, was another factor which presented these participants with difficulty when they had made the decision to exit.

Louise, who had left prostitution a year before the interview when she was 16, had done so because she had met a partner and settled down with him and had a baby. She had never enjoyed being involved in any case and thought it was 'dirty'. From what she told us it was clear that this stigma had 'spoiled' her self identity. The partner with whom she was now living had frequently reminded her of 'what she really was'. She told us,

> He [partner] was trying to make me see how people would look at me and say to me, 'You're nowt but a prostitute. You're not worth bothering with'. He was just trying to make me realise what people would think and look at me as: for what I really am: as a prostitute.

When Louise was asked about what had kept her involved in prostitution she said,

> I wanted to stop then [at 12] but I didn't know where to start. I never got any help from anyone because I didn't know how to ask for it. I've always brought myself up and never asked anyone for help.

The evidence presented in this chapter suggests that the process of getting involved in prostitution is much easier than the process of getting out and that very often the things which propel young people into this way of life are also the very things which keep them involved in it.

SUMMARY

- The evidence in this chapter has suggested that 'child hostile' social policies and labour market conditions can constitute additional barriers to getting out of prostitution for young people. It has shown that, for those under 25 in particular, faced with unemployment or low pay and insecurity in the formal labour market, prostitution provides a route for them to achieve the material standard of living to which they aspire – even though many do not perceive a need for an inordinately large income. There may therefore be a need for government to re-think its policy direction in relation to these areas.

- For the under-25 age group in particular drugs were a significant factor in keeping them involved in prostitution, with the associated economic implications.

- The evidence has once again pointed to the importance of peer group networks in the lives of young people involved in prostitution and shown that, faced with social isolation and rejection by 'straight' society, the friendship networks and relationships they form while involved in prostitution become important in providing them with a sense of belonging and in keeping them involved in that world.

- There is also evidence which suggests that the 'community' to which they belong is sometimes romanticised and that the relationships between people in that community are more contradictory and predatory than they may at first appear.

6

What do young people think might help them to exit?

In this chapter we will consider what participants told us when they were asked what they thought might help them to get out of prostitution. This is not an easy issue to explore. Again, as explained in Chapter 5, it was not always easy for interviewees to distinguish between their experiences as children and as adults. Additionally, many of those interviewed were still working and could only answer hypothetically, while others were reviewing their exit from prostitution in retrospect. The findings presented should therefore be treated with a degree of caution.

We will firstly explore what those who were still involved in prostitution thought might be useful in terms of helping them to get out of prostitution and then look at the factors which had prompted exit amongst those who had already exited at the time of the interviews. The chapter will then examine what the participants told us when asked about the types of interventions they thought might have prevented them from becoming involved in prostitution in the first place.

FACTORS FACILITATING EXIT FOR THOSE STILL INVOLVED

Just over a fifth (11) of participants were unable to say what they thought might help them to get out of prostitution, but, of those who did respond, a range of replies were given and once again there were some marked differences between those who were under 25 and those who were over 25. These differences might be understood as resulting from the changing context of involvement in prostitution for those who had become involved in the past ten to 15 years and those who had become involved prior to this. The factors which those under 25 thought might facilitate their exit can be broadly summarised as help with drugs and/or detoxification programmes and/or improved opportunities for formal employment in the labour market and/or increased welfare benefits. Those over 25, on the other hand, tended to say it was a combination of factors such as money and the provision of emotional support which might help them to get out of prostitution.

HELP WITH DRUGS

As we saw in the previous chapter, a quarter of the under-25 age group said it was their addiction to drugs which prevented them from getting out of prostitution and the same proportion of this age group said it was help with their drug problems which they thought might help them to get out. No one in the over-25 age group gave this reply. As we have seen, those who were using drugs were, for the most part, using heroin, or heroin combined with other drugs such as crack, and in the main they were not interested in drug substitution programmes such as methadone treatment.

Chloe, aged 20, said she was using 'a gram of heroin and £80 worth of crack a day'. At current market rates this was costing her somewhere in the region of £150 per day just to sustain her drug addiction. She related that she had tried methadone programmes in the past but had been thrown off three such programmes because she had tested positive for drugs other than methadone. She said she was not interested in trying another methadone programme. In her opinion the methadone she had been prescribed had not been enough to meet her needs but she felt that if she could have enough prescribed heroin to meet her needs she would probably not work in prostitution. However, she felt it was unrealistic to suppose that she might be prescribed heroin; she was aware that this was not policy and thought it would 'never happen'.

Kate, aged 18, had also tried a methadone programme in the past but said she 'didn't like it' and 'I just jacked it in'. Kate did not know what might help her to get out of prostitution, and did not see herself doing so, but when she was asked directly if she would stop working in prostitution if she could have the heroin she needed prescribed she said she probably would. Again, however, she felt it was unrealistic to suppose that this might really happen. Kate's full story is given on pp. 17–18.

Christine was 20 years old at the time of the interview and had first become involved in prostitution when she was 14 and had gone missing from residential care. She was addicted to heroin at the time of the interview and felt that in order to get out of prostitution she needed 'drug treatment' and a 'drug free environment'. Sally thought that if she could go to a 'detox unit' she might be able to exit from the prostitution. Valerie, Naomi and Lorraine also thought that 'getting off drugs' would be the first step in being able to exit from prostitution.

EDUCATION AND EMPLOYMENT OPPORTUNITIES

Earlier chapters have highlighted the fact that a majority of those interviewed had experienced disrupted educational careers, often characterised by truancy and exclusion. Their consequent lack of educational qualifications obviously had serious consequences in terms of their employment opportunities. Two of the sample had decided, largely on their own initiative, to return to education as a means of quitting prostitution. However, both had lacked support in this and one was on the verge of dropping out of her college course, as she felt that her peers were aware of her background and that she was stigmatised by this.

More often the focus was on finding alternative employment. A quarter of the under-25 age group said that money and/or being able to 'get another job' which paid adequately might help them to get out of prostitution. Some participants had more realistic aspirations for labour market options than others.

Josie, for example, who was 17 at the time of the interview, wanted to be 'a singer in a musical' and said specifically that she wanted to play 'Christine in *Phantom of the Opera*'. She felt that in order to fulfil her ambitions she needed to go to college and that if she could have money to undertake the training she needed she would be able to get out of prostitution. She felt that a grant of about £6000 would be of enormous help to her and that if she could have such a sum she would 'not need to do it [work in prostitution] for the money any more because I would have a start'. However, she felt that the temptation to return to prostitution would always be there if she were ever 'hard up'.

Helen had first become involved at 13 and was 17 at the time of the interview. She said she had not 'worked' in the past two months but she felt that money was 'a big issue' because 'it's something you need every day'. She had often been tempted to return to prostitution by her need for money.

Lisa felt that if she had a job she enjoyed which paid 'decent money' and 'the money to buy the things I want' she would be able to get out of prostitution. Richard and Lawrence also echoed these sentiments. Richard said 'a good job with good pay' would enable him to get out of prostitution while Lawrence said he wanted a 'well paid job'.

Kerry, a 22-year-old male to female transsexual, thought that if she could have a job in which she was accepted for what she was she would be able to get out of prostitution. She felt, however, that she could not obtain employment in the formal labour market until she had undergone surgery to change her sex and would therefore have to remain in prostitution until her sex change was complete.

Nicki was 14 when she was interviewed and was the youngest of the participants to whom we spoke. She felt that if she had received pocket money of £20 per week she might never have become involved in prostitution.

EMOTIONAL SUPPORT

As we saw in the previous chapter, for those who were over 25 at the time of the interview, the friendship networks and sense of belonging which involvement in prostitution provided made getting out of prostitution difficult.

At the time of the interview Liz, aged 42, was trying to exit from prostitution. She had a job in a pub and was only seeing her 'regular punters', but due to lack of money and an absence of friendships beyond the world of prostitution she was finding exit very difficult. She felt that if she had a means of securing the income she needed, and friendships beyond the world of prostitution, she might find it easier to get out completely.

Louise felt that the emotional support she had received from the project with which she was in touch had been important in enabling her to make the decision to get out of prostitution. The project had 'really helped me a lot' in providing her with opportunities to pursue her education and in supplying her with 'options other than working'.

LEAVING PROSTITUTION

As we saw in the previous chapter, just over a third (18) of participants were no longer involved in prostitution at the time of the interview.

Three main issues seemed to be involved: traumatic or difficult events which triggered the decision to exit; a feeling that the individual had 'had enough'; and finding a partner and/or having children.

'TRIGGER' EVENTS

The decision to exit had, on occasion, been preceded by a traumatic event in their personal lives. In Bernadette's case the decision to exit had been informed by the murder of her friend and in Zoe's case by the death of her son. Two of the men had decided to exit after they were diagnosed as being HIV positive. Understandably, such events had caused these individuals to reassess what they were doing and led them to make a conscious decision to move out of prostitution.

'I JUST HAD ENOUGH OF IT'

Gillian was 44 at the time of the interview and had not been involved in prostitution for the past ten years. She had first become involved when she was 15 and had run away from home because she was pregnant and too scared to tell her parents. Her decision to exit from prostitution had been prompted by receiving a prison sentence for non-payment of fines. After she had served her sentence she decided that she could no longer carry on in prostitution. She felt she had simply 'had enough'. She said she still needed the money but was 'just sick of the lifestyle'. Gillian had since married and was living happily at the time of the interview.

Pauline also felt that she had 'just had enough' of the lifestyle when she decided to get out of prostitution. She felt that it had 'taken its toll' on her mentally and that she was, probably irrevocably, damaged by her experiences in prostitution. At the time of the interview she had three part-time jobs and although she found it difficult to make ends meet she was positive she would never return to prostitution. She had decided she would rather be poor than suffer any further abuse through involvement in prostitution.

PARTNERS AND CHILDREN

For several participants the decision to get out of prostitution was prompted by meeting a partner, settling down and having children. In the main it was concern for their children and the desire to provide them with positive role models which prompted the decision to exit.

Liz, who was having difficulty with getting out completely, was concerned that her children were growing up now and 'I wouldn't want them involved in all that'.

Teresa, at 56 the oldest member of the sample, had not been involved in prostitution for the past ten years. She had first become involved when she was 14 and had run away from home to escape from her father's physical and sexual abuse. Her decision to exit was informed by concern for her children: 'I didn't want them to follow in my footsteps', she told us.

Louise had not been involved in prostitution for a year at the time of the interview. She had made the decision to stop when she became pregnant but told us that she had 'wanted to stop for a long time'. She felt that becoming pregnant 'gave me an excuse to stop'. The relationship she had formed was also significant in informing her decision to leave prostitution. She said that she loved her boyfriend and felt that she was 'dirty' and 'cheating on him' while she was still involved in prostitution.

Melanie had also decided to get out of prostitution after forming a relationship, settling down and having children. Her partner did not – and does not – know that she had been involved in prostitution. When she first met her partner she was occasionally still involved in prostitution but when it became clear that the relationship was serious she got out completely. Melanie's full story is given below.

Melanie
Age at time of interview: 34
Age of entry into prostitution: 14

Melanie was the only girl and middle child in a family of five – she had four brothers. She said she was sexually abused for as far back as she could remember by her oldest brother. She thought she was about three when it started and he was about ten or eleven.

When she was about five or six her godfather, who used to babysit for them when the parents were working, started sexually abusing her and he would give her money. She was also abused when she was seven by another man who was known to the godfather but not related. The abuse by the godfather continued for a number of years and when she wanted money for clothes or new trainers and other things she couldn't afford she would get it from the godfather. As a result of this she says, 'You could say I was a prostitute since I was seven'.

She never told anyone about the abuse by any of these people – she was too scared. She thought it might be her fault and that she would get into trouble. She was also frightened about what might happen to the godfather. She told the interviewer that it was the first time she had revealed this abuse to anyone.

Melanie said that when she was growing up they were 'always well dressed and fed' but she always felt left out and never felt as though she belonged. She says it was 'a really weird family'. In particular she always felt that her father was distant and cold towards her. She has learnt as an adult that this was because he had doubts about whether she was really his child.

At 14 she got into an argument with her father who told her to get out of the house. She went to a friend's for a short time and then went to stay with her brother (not the one who had abused her). After this she went home again for a short time but after another argument left and returned to her brother's. After an argument with her brother's girlfriend she had to leave and had nowhere to go. The brother of a friend introduced her to a woman who had her own flat. The woman was about 18. Because she had nowhere to stay the woman let her come to stay with her. This woman was already working as a prostitute and Melanie became involved through her. They worked from the flat. She worked for about three years in total.

She was not working at the time of the interview – she had stopped since she met her partner and had children. Her partner did not know that she used to work as a prostitute and she did not want him to find out.

Melanie thought that if someone had been able to mediate between her and her parents when she was thrown out of home this might have helped her. She also thought if there had been somewhere she could have gone (a safe house or refuge) she probably would never have become involved.

Lesley had successfully left prostitution four years prior to the interview and was now working full time in the formal labour market. Her decision to stop resulted from her concern about the sort of example she might be setting for her children. Although she had now successfully exited from the lifestyle, Lesley spoke about the difficulties of trying to get out. She said she had tried to exit from the lifestyle in the past when her children were young and had taken an office cleaning job. She found, however, that she could not live on the income and had returned to prostitution until she had made the decision to get out for good. Her full story is on pp. 33–4.

WHAT MIGHT HAVE PREVENTED INVOLVEMENT?

Participants were also asked about the things they thought might have prevented them from becoming involved in prostitution in the first place and about the sorts of interventions they thought would have been useful in their lives. A small proportion of participants (six) were unable to say what they thought might have been useful and those over 25 gave this reply twice as often as those under 25. This indicates that those in the younger age group have a clearer idea of the types of assistance they might usefully be provided with than those in the older age group. Several participants found it easier to say what they had not found useful rather than what they thought might have been helpful. For example, one participant had been placed in an observation and assessment centre by social services, and experienced this as punitive rather than helpful. A small group of six participants were quite certain that there was nothing anyone could have done to prevent them from becoming involved. In a minority of cases, individuals had been forced into prostitution by another person and they felt that no-one could have done anything about the fear that had coerced them. As one participant told us, 'fear is a terrible thing'. Others said they were 'wilful' and would not have listened to anyone at the time. Those who were under 25 at the time of the interview said twice as frequently as those who were over 25 that they would not have listened to anyone at the time and that there was nothing anyone could have done to help them.

Amongst those who could articulate what they felt would have helped them, interventions into their family situations, help with drug problems and being warned of the dangers involved in what they were doing, were most frequently cited as things which might have prevented their involvement.

FAMILY SITUATIONS

Just over a quarter (13) of the entire sample said they felt that earlier intervention into their home situations, opportunities for mediation between themselves and their parents and/or being loved and cared for 'properly' might have prevented them from becoming involved. Those who were under 25 tended to give this response slightly more frequently than those who were over 25; just over a quarter (eight) of the younger age group thought this would have helped them compared to approximately a fifth (five) of the older age group.

Jenny, aged 17, had experienced a lot of conflict with her mother when she was younger. She said she was 'always blamed for all the naughty things my brother did' as well as all the 'naughty things' she did herself. She was 'always being grounded' by her mother and had started truanting from school, 'that's when I started getting into trouble'. She ran away from home at 15 and became involved in prostitution. Jenny said that when she ran away 'me mum just left me to get on with it' and that nobody bothered to look for her. She was 'living from hand to mouth or whatever you call it'. Jenny felt that both her family and social services could have done more to support her during this troubled period of her youth. She felt that, 'if my mum hadn't been so heartless and sat me down and talked to me' she probably would not have run away from home and consequently would not have become involved in prostitution. She felt that social services 'could have done a lot to help me. They could have put me in a hostel – even a safe house. I got myself into a safe house'. She now has very negative views of social workers and social services, and stated flatly during interview, 'Social services? If I ever saw them I'd 'it 'em'.

Karen, aged 18, had also had an unhappy home life. She said her mother was always out, 'going drinking', and had never paid her attention or shown her any affection. She never had help with her homework and always had to get herself ready for school. Karen's mother threw her out of her home when she was 13; she returned a short while later but from this time she frequently stayed away from home for periods of time. After she had returned home she was sent on an 'anger management course' which she found totally inappropriate. She said that her problems had started in her family and that if her mother had been 'more supportive or understanding, if she had treated me better' maybe she would never have become involved in prostitution in the first place.

Kate, also aged 18, had also had a very unhappy relationship with her mother which resulted, primarily, from her being sent away to live with her grandparents, against her wishes, when she was six. As a result of this Kate never felt that her mother wanted her. She returned to live with her mother when she was 12 but she still felt unwanted and felt that her mother either would not, or could not, adequately explain her reasons for having sent her away in the first place. She felt that she had 'the right to some answers' but was never given any. When she was asked what she felt might have been useful in preventing her from becoming involved in prostitution she said she just wanted her mother to say, ' "Don't go out tonight, stay at home", but she never did ye know'. Kate did have a social worker but said, 'I just weren't interested' because in her perception all the social worker had wanted to talk about was her relationship with her mother. Kate said she was 'sick of people telling me to stop blaming my mum for fucking up my life'. Kate's full story is on pp. 17–18.

Christine was taken into care when she was three as a result of experiencing physical and sexual abuse in the home at the hands of her stepfather. When she was asked what might have helped her to avoid becoming involved in prostitution, she said, 'Being treated with respect and being loved would have stopped me from getting involved in the first place'.

Rachel was placed in the care of the local authority by her mother when she was 15 because she had been refusing to go to school and had been getting into trouble through stealing and other criminal activity. She had been suffering physical abuse at the hands of her stepfather and had previously been raped by her father but had not disclosed this abuse to anyone and it was not the reason for her entry into care. Rachel felt that she might have avoided becoming involved in prostitution if her mother had 'showed me more love and give me more support. No-one was giving me the attention I needed'.

Peter thought that if his father had been more understanding about his emerging homosexuality he would have been able to remain in the family home and would not have become involved in prostitution. He also felt that if there had been somewhere for him to go when his father threw him out this would have helped. However, he did not think that a refuge or hostel place alone would have prevented his entry into prostitution because he would not have had any money and would have 'needed to do something' in order to get some.

SOMEONE TO TALK TO

A small number of participants felt that if there had been someone for them to talk to about the emotional difficulties they were confronting when they were younger they might not have become involved in prostitution.

Naomi's story was given on p. 58. She had had a fairly happy and stable home life until she was about 12. At this age she was told that she was actually adopted and that the man whom she had always considered to be her uncle was in fact her father. Finding this out was a traumatic experience for Naomi and she started truanting from school, 'smoking heroin' and 'getting into trouble'. At 15 her adoptive parents sent her to live in a hostel and shortly afterwards her adoptive mother died. Naomi then progressed to injecting heroin and began working in prostitution to provide the money for her drugs. When she was asked what might have helped her to avoid becoming involved in prostitution, Naomi said that if she had had a social worker or 'someone to talk to' about finding out that she was adopted and her adoptive mother dying she might never have become involved in prostitution.

Elaine also felt that if she had been able to talk to someone when she was younger she might not have become involved in prostitution. Elaine was 30 at the time of the interview. At 16 she left home, because she did not get on with her father, and became involved in a relationship with an older man. After a month the man began to mistreat her; he took her to London, forced her to start working as a prostitute and took all her money from her. When she was asked what she felt anyone could have done at this time to help her, she said she was unaware at the time of any services that might have been able to provide her with support and that she would have been too frightened anyway to approach them. However, Elaine felt that if there had been someone she could have trusted enough to tell them what was happening to her, this might have helped her.

PEER EDUCATION

Participants in both age groups felt that if there had been someone who could have warned them about the dangers of what they were getting involved in, they might have been 'put off' becoming involved in prostitution. However, they were not keen to be 'preached at' and they felt that the best person to provide such advice would be 'someone who's been through it themselves and who understands what you're going through'. There was a perception that people who had not 'been through it' could not understand the experience and would not be in a position to offer such advice. Several participants expressed the view that they would not be willing to take advice from anyone who had not had first-hand experience of prostitution.

REFUGE

Five participants said that if there had been somewhere, such as a refuge, for them to go when they left home they would probably never have become involved in prostitution. Four of these participants were in the over-25 age group and one was under 25. This finding needs to be interpreted in terms of the different provision which might have been available for those in the older age group when they first became involved in prostitution compared with those who became involved in the more recent past. Although the consensus amongst the older participants was that it was much more dangerous for young people becoming involved in prostitution today compared to when they were young – because of drugs and violence – they also thought that generally there was much more help available for young people today. The older participants tended to say that they felt provision of support for those who might become involved now had improved a great deal compared to when they were young and first became involved themselves. They felt especially that there were no projects or refuges to which they could turn for help when they were younger.

HELP WITH DRUGS

We have seen that seven participants said explicitly that they entered prostitution because they wanted money for drugs and four of this group felt that if they had been able to get help with their drug problems they would not have become involved in prostitution in the first place.

FACILITATING EXIT

The evidence presented in this chapter suggests that, in terms of facilitating exit from prostitution, different interventions are appropriate for different age groups. To facilitate exit for those who are under 25, it is important to provide realistic alternatives and opportunities in the formal labour market and, for those in this age group who struggle with addictions, appropriate drug treatment programmes are essential. While a return to education did not feature strongly in the accounts of those interviewed, obtaining some form of qualification or entering training may provide an incentive for those who aspire to earning more in the formal labour market.

We have also seen that several participants made the decision to exit from prostitution when they had formed stable relationships and had children of their own. This suggests that it is important to support those who are involved until such time as they feel ready to make the decision to get out. As we have seen, the emotional support which these young people have received from the projects with which they are in contact has been an important source of strength to them and has facilitated their decision to get out in some instances. Such projects were non-judgmental in their approach, and supported individuals regardless of whether they were intending to exit, but also offered opportunities in, for example, education. For some of those interviewed, this had helped restore some of their self-esteem and offered the possibility of making some change in their lives.

In terms of preventing entry to prostitution, the participants told us that interventions into their family situations, having someone to talk to, being warned of the dangers involved by peers who have managed to get out of prostitution, the provision of refuge and appropriate treatment facilities for those with drug problems, are all important factors. In the following chapter we will explore the implications for policy and practice of what our participants have told us.

SUMMARY

- It is difficult to predict the factors that will trigger exit from prostitution. Personal life events, changing circumstances such as having children, and the broader social policy context all play a part.

- The under-25 age group particularly need to be supported with appropriate drug treatment programmes and provided with opportunities for training and employment in the formal economy and/or with increased welfare benefits. In addition, there is a need to continue to provide this age group with emotional support and opportunities for returning to study through the projects with which they are in touch.

- The evidence in this chapter also suggests that there is a need to remain vigilant about family situations and to provide opportunities for mediation services between parents and children. As Melanie told us, 'It's not just us who need help, it's our parents too'.

CHAPTER 7

Implications for policy and practice

This study has demonstrated the types of suffering, abuse, exploitation and pain the participants had endured in the course of their lives – in some cases in the very short span of their lives. We have seen that many had experienced conflict or abuse in their early lives, that a substantial proportion had experience of being looked after in local authority residential care and that many had interrupted or prematurely terminated educational careers. This study has shown that different motivations led these participants into prostitution: some were motivated by their need to survive in the context of going missing from home or care, some by the desire to achieve a standard of living which they would not otherwise be able to achieve, a small proportion were coerced to enter prostitution and a smaller proportion again were motivated to obtain money to feed their drug addictions. It has also become evident that young people appeared to be entering prostitution at very young ages and that peer group influences were more important than coercion in leading the people in this sample into prostitution. This highlights the fact that child prostitution is a multi-faceted problem, and the young people involved should not be viewed as a homogeneous group. Understanding these different motivations is also important if we are to develop appropriate responses and effective solutions to this problem (Ayre and Barrett, 1999).

We have seen that violence was central to the experiences of young people in prostitution and that drug use was relatively high amongst the whole group but particularly high amongst the under-25s. A majority of participants were not in favour of decriminalising prostitution for those under 18 although they were in favour of severe penalties for the men who abuse young people through prostitution. The study has also demonstrated that the strategies many participants employed to avoid detection by the authorities made them difficult for helping agencies to identify and target.

The report has also demonstrated that labour market and welfare policies in relation to young people appeared to militate against them getting out of prostitution once involved, and that the sense of 'belonging' and/or empowerment which many derived from involvement in prostitution made it difficult to exit. As we have seen, for a small proportion of the sample, particularly in the under-25 age group, their dependence on addictive drugs kept them involved in prostitution.

We have also seen that, in terms of helping them to get out of prostitution, participants in this study thought that opportunities in the labour market, emotional support and help with drug problems would help them. In terms of preventing entry to prostitution, those interviewed felt that interventions into abusive family situations, having someone to talk to, peer education, refuges and support with drugs problems were important factors.

The findings in this report therefore serve to emphasise the complexity of the problem of young people who become involved in prostitution. It demonstrates that their entry into prostitution is influenced by a constellation of social and emotional factors such as poverty, abuse, low self-esteem, lack of educational qualifications and opportunities in the formal labour market, peer group influences and, sometimes, the experience of being looked after away from home. Responses to the problem therefore need to address and acknowledge the inter-relationship between these different factors if effective and meaningful interventions are to be developed.

In this chapter we will tentatively explore the implications of the findings of this study, both in terms of how agencies can help prevent young people from becoming involved in prostitution, and also how support can best be given after individuals have entered prostitution. It is important to emphasise again that this is a modest study, and that this is an area of research where much is still unknown. Four areas of policy and practice will be considered: statutory and voluntary provision of services to meet the needs of young people involved in prostitution; the law and policing; education; the labour market and welfare benefits. We end with a brief summary of key recommendations for each area.

STATUTORY AND VOLUNTARY AGENCIES

The Children Act 1989 places on local authorities certain statutory obligations to respond to the needs of vulnerable young people and/or young people at risk. Section 17 of the Act 'requires the local authority to safeguard and protect the welfare of children in their area who are in need'; Section 44 allows for the child or young person to be made the subject of an Emergency Protection Order if the social services department considers that the child is suffering 'significant harm' and 'needs to be moved to a safe place or remain in one'; Section 47 places on local authorities the duty to 'make enquiries where they have reasonable cause to suspect that a child is suffering or likely to suffer significant harm' so that they can decide on an appropriate course of action to 'safeguard and promote' the child's welfare.

Yet, as Ayre and Barrett (1999) have argued, local authorities and social services departments have, in the past, been disinclined to accept that young people involved in prostitution are vulnerable or 'at risk', and previous research has shown that responses of social services agencies to the problems of young people involved in prostitution have, on occasion, left much to be desired (Jesson *et al.*, 1991; Barrett, 1997). New government guidelines (Home Office/Department of Health, 1998), however, clearly define young people involved in prostitution as vulnerable or 'at risk' and require local authorities and social services departments to respond to them as such. These new guidelines require local authorities and social services departments to work in conjunction with other agencies, such as education, health, policing, youth services and voluntary organisations, to ensure the welfare of the child. It is to be hoped that the practices which are informed by these new guidelines will provide young people involved in prostitution with the care and protection they need. These messages have been reiterated in response to Sir William Utting's review of safeguards for children living away from home (Utting, 1997; Department of Health and others, 1998). Consultation is also currently taking place regarding some aspects of child protection and it has been suggested that area child protection committees should be encouraged to develop protocols for responding to child prostitution in their areas (Department of Health and others, 1998). Other government initiatives such as Quality Protects also emphasise the importance of a multi-agency approach to protecting children and improving the outcomes for those who are especially vulnerable (Department of Health, 1998). These are encouraging developments.

The evidence presented in this report demonstrates that the trauma of abusive experiences in young people's lives can leave them feeling worthless, unloved and unwanted when they are young adults and suggests that, as Browne and Falshaw (1998) argue, there is a need to develop services which provide young people involved in prostitution with opportunities for counselling and the chance to explore their own victimisation. Additionally, there is a need to make these services available while young people are still on the street (Browne and Falshaw, 1998) or involved in prostitution.

Evidence from earlier research suggests that young people on the street often respond better to non-traditional services than to other types of service provision (Browne and Falshaw, 1998; McNeish, 1998; Crosby and Barrett, 1999). This suggests that the development of outreach and 'street based' services, which are located in the vicinities in which they work, would provide a particularly useful way forward. Indeed, all of the participants were in touch with such services but the majority did not make use of other services beyond these particular projects.

Browne and Falshaw (1998) have argued that The Children's Society projects in Birmingham, Leeds, Manchester and Gwent provide examples of good practice in their work with young people who are involved in prostitution. However, they noted that these projects are geared towards short-term, crisis intervention rather than the provision of long-term support – for example, counselling, educational facilities and careers advice – which young people involved in prostitution might require if they are to be enabled to change their way of life. Many agencies and projects which offer support to those involved in prostitution do not aim specifically to provide services for young people, and, indeed, of those projects through which participants for this study were accessed, only one specifically targeted its services for young people. The evidence presented in this report suggests that there is a need for more projects which are centred on young people.

The evidence also suggests that projects need to take a holistic view of the young people with whom they are in touch and should be geared up to respond to a range of complex needs and multi-dimensional problems which the young people may be confronting in their lives. These may include any or all of the following: abuse, homelessness, violent relationships, lack of money, drug use, lack of qualifications, lack of self-esteem, social isolation and problems associated with child-rearing. Projects which aim to provide services to young people involved in prostitution need to be able to offer long-term support and help in a variety of areas in the young person's life and might include educational facilities, support with child-rearing, opportunities for counselling, and support with drug problems (Browne and Falshaw, 1998; Crosby and Barrett, 1999).

This study has highlighted a need for projects to offer support for people under the age of 25 with drug problems. These might include detoxification programmes, needle exchange programmes and, perhaps more radically, controlled prescription of the drugs they require. Projects might also usefully offer facilities for legal representation and advocacy and advice in relation to welfare benefits, housing and sexual health services.

The finding that many of the participants in the study had experienced being looked after in local authority care at some point in their lives indicates that there is a need to think again about the support systems which are available to young people leaving care as well as what might be happening to them when they are being looked after. Farmer and Pollock (1998) have shown that children who were involved or 'on the fringes of involvement' in prostitution while they were being looked after had the worst behavioural outcomes of all of those being looked after who were studied. They found that placement far away from the young person's social networks was the most useful response to the problem. In situations where the young person is removed from existing social networks, peer mentoring schemes might usefully be developed which would provide advice and guidance to divert them away from prostitution. Such mentoring schemes have been found to be effective in other work with young people (Department of Health, 1996). However, geographically distant placements will not be the answer for all, and consideration also needs to be given to the combination of young people placed in a residential unit at any one time (Department of Health, 1998). It is also important that carers are informed if the young person has already had involvement in prostitution, so that appropriate care planning and supervision can take place.

In the light of what participants themselves told us about the importance of peer group influences in leading them into prostitution, and what previous research has revealed about the value of peer education in young people's lives (Department of Health, 1996; O'Neill *et al.*, 1995), the authors would recommend that projects, and other agencies concerned to provide solutions to this problem, develop peer education schemes in order that such formal schemes would undermine the informal peer education which currently serves to draw young people into prostitution.

THE LAW AND POLICING

We have seen in this report that the application of the criminal law exacerbates the problems confronting young people involved in prostitution. Although not the only factor, frequent encounters with the police and criminal justice agencies can encourage them to move around and adopt false identities in an effort to avoid detection and therefore poses extra difficulties for those agencies which are concerned to develop and provide solutions for them.

New government guidelines issued by the Home Office/Department of Health (1998) urge the police to respond to juveniles involved in prostitution in terms of the Children Act 1989 rather than in terms of the criminal law; that is, in conjunction with other agencies, it is recommended that the police respond to 'all' young people in prostitution as 'children in need, who may be suffering or may be likely to suffer, significant harm'. The guidelines recommend that 'the primary law enforcement effort must be against abusers', and that children drawn into prostitution *'should be protected from further abuse'* (our italics). However, the guidelines also allow that 'it may be appropriate for those who persistently and voluntarily return to prostitution to enter the criminal justice system in the way that other young offenders do'.

This means that in practice we are left with the contradictory and highly unsatisfactory situation of trying to protect young people from further abuse through prostitution while criminalising them for continuing to put themselves in situations where they will suffer such abuse. Our evidence, and evidence from other sources, suggests that it is precisely those who are most psychologically and emotionally damaged and most materially deprived – the most vulnerable and 'in need' – who will continue to put themselves in such situations and to whom, we might suggest, it is most inappropriate to apply the criminal law (O'Neill, 1997; Pitts, 1997; O'Connell-Davidson, 1998). Our report has shown that while they may persist in prostitution their return to it results from a *highly constrained agency* rather than from a free agency and in this sense it cannot be considered as 'voluntary'. According to the Oxford English Dictionary, 'voluntary' is defined as 'done, acting, able to act, of one's own free will; purposed, intentional, not constrained'. Given the constraints of their economic and emotional circumstances which have been described above, this definition can hardly be applied to these young people.

The evidence presented in this report suggests that there is a need for the police to establish relationships of trust with young people involved in prostitution so that when they are the victims of crimes, such as rape and assault, they will be willing to report such crimes to the police. In short, the police have a duty to ensure that the same civilities are extended to young people involved in prostitution as they would be to any other member of the public.

The new government guidelines recommend that the police concentrate their efforts on those who abuse young people through prostitution and ensure that young people are protected from them. This has been advocated by agencies concerned to protect young people from abuse through prostitution (Lee and O'Brien, 1995; Swann, 1998) and is a measure which is to be welcomed by practitioners in this field.

EDUCATION

The evidence from this study has shown that nearly half the sample became involved in prostitution when they were 14 or younger. This indicates that in schools across the country there are young people who may be pupils by day and 'workers' by night. Although teachers may be unwilling to accept that their charges are being abused through prostitution (Bowen, 1997), the evidence from this small study clearly demonstrates that they are. This places a particular onus on teachers to be vigilant about young people and indicates a need for teachers to be 'aware of the outline of their pupils' social lives' (Bowen, 1997) and to be aware of the sorts of peer associations and networks of friends their pupils may be involved with. There is a need for teachers to respond with non-judgmental attitudes to young people involved in prostitution so that these pupils might feel able to confide in their teachers about their experiences beyond the classroom (Bowen, 1997).

However, many of those interviewed had been 'out of school', whether as a result of exclusion or extended absence, from an early age. Prevention of prostitution must therefore also involve preventative action in relation to these negative educational outcomes. It is perhaps unfortunate that so much of the debate on school exclusion has seen this as a male problem on account of the disproportionate numbers of boys involved (Brodie, 1998); consideration also needs to be given to the risks at which young women are placed. The Government's Social Exclusion Unit has already published targets for the reduction of the numbers of exclusions taking place and for the introduction of full-time and appropriate education for all those out of school (Social Exclusion Unit, 1998). Increasing emphasis has also been given to the importance of early intervention when behavioural problems emerge within the classroom. These are encouraging developments with potential benefits for young people at risk of involvement in prostitution.

The onus is also on teachers and the education service to follow up absences from school rigorously: that so many of the people interviewed said they 'just stopped going' to school, in some cases when they were as young as 12 or 13, and/or that 'no-one bothered about it' suggests that many of these young people have been failed by the education service they received. It is to be hoped that in future teachers' duty to inform parents about pupils' absence will mean that such absences will no longer go undetected.

For those young people already alienated from the education system, there is a case for developing educational 'outreach' services which provide opportunities for learning away from the school environment. Such facilities had been developed, in conjunction with the local youth service, education service and educational welfare officers, at one of the projects through which participants for this study were accessed. The young people concerned found this an invaluable service and were extremely grateful for the opportunities it had provided them with for pursuing their educational careers.

If young people are to be prevented from becoming involved in prostitution, schools, teachers and the curriculum need to address the problem more centrally for all three are crucial to any programme of prevention (Bowen, 1997). Recent evidence has suggested that schools, working in conjunction with the family and other agencies such as the police and social services departments, serve as an ideal base for the provision of other services (Ball, 1998).

THE LABOUR MARKET AND WELFARE

The evidence presented in this report, as well as evidence from other research (Green, 1992; Green *et al.*, 1997), indicates that the un-intended consequences of labour market policies and inadequate levels of welfare benefits play a part in keeping young people involved in prostitution. The evidence suggests that the Government needs to review, with some urgency, its policies in relation to the position of young people in the labour market.

We have seen in the introduction that one child in three now lives in poverty in Britain (Oppenheim and Lister, 1996; Barrett, 1997), and that young adults experience twice the average rate of unemployment while those who have jobs are five times as likely to be paid below half the male average wage than older workers (Joseph Rowntree Foundation, 1998).

The evidence from this report suggests that many of the young people interviewed might be diverted from involvement in prostitution if they were provided with realistic alternatives in the formal labour market. This would involve making them subject to the provisions of minimum wage legislation.

Additionally, for those unable to obtain employment and who are under 18 years of age, their entitlement to welfare benefits, paid at the same rate as those over 25 years of age, needs to be restored so that young people are not discriminated against on the basis of their age. After all, it costs no less to live in an area when one is 17 than when one is 27. To reduce entitlement to welfare on the basis of age tells young people quite clearly that our society values them less than adults. This is a message that vulnerable and already under-valued young people do not need to hear.

That so many of the participants in this study were driven by eco-nomic motivation to enter prostitution before they were old enough to be legally employed in the formal labour market suggests a need to think seriously about the introduction of a system whereby young people would have independent access to an income before they are old enough to work. This might be something like a modified Citizen's Income which would be paid directly to the child from the moment of birth until s/he reaches 18. This might take the form of a credit rather than a cash payment. Those young people who find themselves in crisis in their families would be able to access this credit pool if they were to leave home before they reached 18. This would be a universal, rather than a means tested benefit, which would benefit all young people, rich and poor alike but it would be of greatest benefit to those who are most vulnerable. Those who did not leave home before they were 18 would receive their credit upon reaching this age. It would of course be important to ensure that proper systems were in place so that vulnerable young people could not be forced by another, adult or child, to access their credit pool.

The report has shown that young people involved in prostitution are the victims of a power imbalance which exists between adults and young people in contemporary society. It has shown that they are the victims of abuse, violence and exploitation, not only by the adults who abuse them through prostitution but also by other institutions, such as the family, the education system, the law, social services and the economy, which have failed to meet their needs. In this sense we may begin to understand young people's involvement in prostitution as the result of long-term and entrenched institutional neglect. This understanding and the evidence presented in this report demonstrate that nothing short of national, long-term, multi-agency responses to this problem will suffice if young people are to be prevented from entering prostitution and if they are to be enabled to extricate themselves from such involvement once it has occurred.

KEY RECOMMENDATIONS

VOLUNTARY AND STATUTORY SERVICES
- There is a need for street-based, young-person centred services which provide opportunities for counselling, a chance to explore victimisation and offer long-term support, by providing education

facilities; careers guidance; help with housing and welfare benefits; help with drugs and childcare; detoxification facilities and needle exchange schemes.

- In accordance with Home Office/Department of Health guidelines (1998), local authorities and social services departments should work in conjunction with police, education, health and youth services and voluntary organisations to ensure the welfare of the child.

- Thought should be given to the combinations of young people being looked after together. Carers should be informed of any involvement in prostitution. Peer mentoring and peer education schemes should be provided.

LAW AND POLICING

- In accordance with Home Office/Department of Health guidelines (1998), young people should be provided with care and protection under the Children Act 1989 not conviction by criminal law.

- Relations of trust should be established with young people so that they feel free to report crimes committed against them.

- Efforts should be concentrated against those who abuse young people.

EDUCATION

- Teachers need to be vigilant about pupils' lives – to follow up absences and ensure that satisfactory explanations are provided.

- Schools should aim for a reduction in school exclusions and early intervention when behavioural problems are manifest in the classroom.

- There is a need for educational outreach and opportunities for learning away from the school environment.

- Problems of young people and prostitution should be addressed more centrally by schools, teachers and the curriculum.

LABOUR MARKET AND WELFARE PROVISION

- There should be realistic opportunities for young people in the labour market. Young people should be subject to the provision of minimum wage legislation.

- Previous levels of benefit should be restored so that young people are not discriminated against on the basis of age.

- A system should be developed to provide a means of access to an independent income for young people.

Appendix

SUMMARY OF INTERVIEWEES (IN ORDER OF INTERVIEW)

Name	Age at interview	Age of entry to prostitution	Continued involvement?
Susan	26	16	Yes
Bernadette	30	15	No
Jenny	17	15	Yes
Maureen	43	17	Yes
Rose	38	17	Yes
Alison	27	17	Yes
Sheila	28	12	No
Elaine	30	16	Yes
Valerie	23	17	Yes
Sally	24	15	Yes
Tracey	22	16	Yes
Zoe	24	16	No
Anita	37	16	Yes
Dawn	24	15	Yes
Kate	18	12	Yes
Neil	20	13	No
Lesley	40	13	No
Janet	47	17	No
Kathy	37	16	Yes
Pete	26	14	No
Richard	25	14	Yes
Sandra	38	13	Yes
Kim	17	11	Yes
Lisa	18	12	Yes

Name	Age at interview	Age of entry to prostitution	Continued involvement?
Lawrence	18	13	Yes
Teresa	56	14	No
Melanie	34	14	No
Gillian	44	15	No
Claire	39	14	Yes
Pauline	48	15	No
Liz	42	13	Yes
Marie	24	15	Yes
Jackie	26	13	Yes
Naomi	18	15	Yes
Chloe	20	16	Yes
Josie	17	14	Yes
Nicki	14	13	No
Helen	17	13	No
Karen	18	14	No
Rachel	18	14	Yes
Louise	17	11	No
Mary	39	13	Yes
Carol	37	13	Yes
Kerry	22	17	Yes
Denise	24	17	No
Lorraine	18	17	Yes
Joan	49	16	No
Tina	23	15	No
Julie	28	14	Yes
Christine	20	14	Yes

References

Abrahams, C., Mungall, R. (1992) *Runaways: Exploding the Myths.* London: National Children's Homes.

Adams, N., Carter, C., Carter, S., Lopez-Jones, N., Mitchell, C. (1997) 'Demystifying child prostitution: a street view.' In D. Barrett (ed.) *Child Prostitution in Britain: Dilemmas and Practical Responses.* London: The Children's Society.

Aitchison, P., O'Brien, R. (1997) 'Redressing the balance: the legal context of child prostitution.' In D. Barrett (ed.) *Child Prostitution in Britain: Dilemmas and Practical Responses.* London: The Children's Society.

Allbeson, J. (1985) 'Seen but not heard: young people.' In S. Ward (ed.) *DHSS in Crisis: Social Security under Pressure and under Review.* London: Child Poverty Action Group.

Andrieu-Sanz. R., Vasquez-Anton, K. (1989) 'Young women prostitutes in Bilbao.' In M. Cain (ed.) *Growing Up Good: Policing the Behaviour of Girls in Europe.* London: Sage.

Armstrong, E. G. (1983) 'Pondering pandering.' *Deviant Behaviour* **4** (2): 203–17.

Ayre, P., Barrett, D. (1999, forthcoming) 'Young people and prostitution: An end to the beginning?' *Children and Society.*

Ball, J. (1998) *School Inclusion; The School, the Family and the Community.* York: Joseph Rowntree Foundation.

Barbaret, R., Barrett, D., O'Neill, M. (1995) 'Young people and prostitution: No respecter of boundaries in North Western Europe.' *Social Work in Europe* **2** (2), pp. 44–5.

Barclay, Sir Peter. (1995) *Inquiry into Income and Wealth*, 1. York: Joseph Rowntree Foundation.

Barnard, M., McKeganey, N., Bloor, M. (1990) 'A risky business.' *Community Care*, 5 July.

Barrett, D. (1994a) 'Social work on the street: Responding to juvenile prostitution in Amsterdam, London and Paris.' *Social Work in Europe*, 1 (2), pp. 29–32.

Barrett, D. (1994b) 'Stop the bus, we want to get on.' *The Guardian*, 10 August.

Barrett, D. (1995) 'Child prostitution.' *Highlight*, no. 135, London: National Children's Bureau.

Barrett, D. (1997) 'Introduction' and 'Conclusion'. In D. Barrett (ed.) *Child Prostitution in Britain: Dilemmas and Practical Responses.* London: The Children's Society.

Berridge, D., Brodie, I. (1998) *Children's Homes Revisited.* London: Jessica Kingsley.

Blom, M., van den Berg, T. (1989) 'A typology of the life and work styles of "heroin prostitutes": from a male career model to a feminized career model.' In M. Cain (ed.) *Growing Up Good: Policing the Behaviour of Girls in Europe.* London: Sage.

Bourgois, P. (1996) *In Search of Respect: Selling Crack in El Barrio.* Cambridge: Cambridge University Press.

Bowen, D. (1997) 'Child prostitution: An educational perspective.' In D. Barrett (ed.) *Child Prostitution in Britain: Dilemmas and Practical Responses.* London: The Children's Society.

Brain, T. (1998) 'Is the game up?' *Policing Today*, March.

Brain, T., Duffin, T., Anderson, S., Parchment, P. (1998) *Child Prostitution: A Report on the ACPO Guidelines and the pilot studies in Wolverhampton and Nottinghamshire.* Gloucestershire Constabulary.

Brannen, J. (1992) *Mixing methods: qualitative and quantitative methods.* Aldershot: Avebury.

British Youth council (1992) *The Time of Your Life? The Truth about being Young in 90's Britain.* London: British Youth Council.

Brodie, I. (1998) 'Exclusion from school.' *Highlight*, no. 161. London: National Children's Bureau.

Browne, K., Falshaw, L. (1998) 'Street children in the UK: A case of abuse and neglect.' *Child Abuse Review*, 7, pp. 241–53.

Coffield, F., Borrill, C., Marshall, S. (1986) *Growing Up at the Margins: Young Adults in the North East*. Milton Keynes: Open University Press.

Coles, B. (1995) *Youth and Social Policy: Youth Citizenship and Young Careers*. London: UCL Press.

Corby, B. (1997) 'The mistreatment of young people.' In J. Roche and S. Tucker (eds) *Youth in Society*, London: Sage.

Crosby, S., Barrett, D., (1999. forthcoming) 'Poverty, drugs and youth prostitution: A case study of service providers' practical response.' In A. Marlow and J. Pitts (eds) *Managing Drugs and Young People*. Lyme Regis: Russell House Publishing.

Curren, E., Sinclair, S. (unpublished 1998) *Sexual Health Outreach Project Report*. Harbour Centre Alcohol and Drug Advisory Service, Plymouth.

Davies, P., Feldman, R. (1997) 'Prostitute men now.' In G. Scambler and A. Scambler (eds) *Rethinking Prostitution: Purchasing Sex in the 1990's*. London: Routledge.

Davis, N. (1978) 'Prostitution: identity, career and legal economic enterprise.' In J. Henslin and E. Sagarin (eds) *The Sociology of Sex*. New York: Schocken Books.

Dean, H. (1997) 'Underclassed or undermined? Young people and social citizenship.' In R. MacDonald (ed.) *Youth, the 'Underclass' and Social Exclusion*. London: Routledge.

Dean, H., Barrett, D. (1996) 'Unrespectable research and researching the unrespectable.' In H. Dean (ed.) *Ethics and Social Policy Research*. Luton: University of Luton Press in conjunction with the Social Policy Association.

Dean, H., Melrose, M. (1996) 'Unravelling citizenship: the significance of social security benefit fraud.' *Critical Social Policy*, 48 (16): 3–32.

Dean, H., with Melrose, M. (1998) *Poverty, Riches and Social Citizenship*. Basingstoke: MacMillan.

Dean, H., Melrose, M. (1999) 'Easy pickings or hard profession? Begging as an economic activity.' *Begging and Street Level Economic Activity*. Bristol: Policy Press.

Dean, H., Taylor-Gooby, P. (1992) *Dependency Culture: The Explosion of a Myth*. Hemel Hempstead: Harvester Wheatsheaf.

Department of Health (1996) *Focus on Teenagers.* London: HMSO.

Department of Health (1998) *Quality Protects: Framework for Action.* London: Department of Health.

Department of Health and others (1998) *Government Response to Children's Safeguards Review.* London: HMSO.

Dorn, N., South, N. (1987) *A Land Fit For Heroin? Drug Policies, Prevention and Practice.* Basingstoke: MacMillan.

Douglas, A., Gilroy, R. (1994) 'Young women and homelessness.' In R. Gilroy and R. Woods (eds) *Housing Women.* London: Routledge.

Edwards, S. M. (1992) 'Prostitutes: Victims of law, social policy and organised crime.' In P. Carlen and A. Worrall (eds) *Gender, Crime and Justice.* Buckingham: Open University Press.

Edwards, S. M. (1998) 'Abused and exploited – young girls in prostitution: A consideration of the legal issues.' In *Whose Daughter Next? Children Abused through Prostitution.* Essex: Barnardo's.

English Collective of Prostitutes (1997) 'Campaigning for legal change.' In G. Scambler and A. Scambler (eds) *Rethinking Prostitution: Purchasing Sex in the 1990's.* London: Routledge.

Farmer, E., Pollock, S. (1998) 'Sexually abused and abusing children in substitute care.' *Caring for Children Away from Home: Messages from Research.* Department of Health. Chichester: John Wiley and Sons.

Faugier, J., Sergeant, M. (1997) 'Boyfriends, "pimps" and clients.' In G. Scambler and A. Scambler (eds) *Rethinking Prostitution: Purchasing Sex in the 1990's.* London: Routledge.

Faugier, J., Hayes, C., Butterworth, C. A. (1992) *Drug using Prostitutes, their Health Care Needs, and their Clients.* Department of Nursing, University of Manchester, Manchester.

France, A. (1996) 'Youth citizenship in the 1990's.' *Youth and Policy,* no. 53, pp. 28–44.

Green, J. (1992) *It's No Game: Responding to the Needs of Young Women at Risk or Involved in Prostitution.* Leicester: National Youth Agency.

Green, J., Mulroy, S., O'Neill, M. (1997) 'Young people and prostitution from a youth service perspective.' In D. Barrett (ed.) *Child Prostitution in Britain: Dilemmas and Practical Responses.* London: The Children's Society.

Groocock, V. (1992) 'Streets ahead.' *Social Work Today* **23** (5).

Hardman, K. (1997) 'A social work group for prostituted women with children.' *Social Work with Groups*, **20** (1), pp. 19–31.

Hewlett, S. A. (1993) *Child Neglect in Rich Nations*. Florence, Italy and New York: UNICEF.

Hills, J. (1995) *Inquiry into Income and Wealth*, vol. 2. York: Joseph Rowntree Foundation.

Homan, R. (1991) *The Ethics of Social Research*. Harlow: Longman.

Home Office/Department of Health (1998) *Guidance on Children involved in Prostitution*. London: Home Office/Department of Health.

Hutson, S., Liddiard, M. (1994) *Youth Homelessness: The Construction of a Social Issue*. Basingstoke: MacMillan.

Jesson, J. (1991) *Young Women in Care: The Social Services Care System and Juvenile Prostitution*. Birmingham City Council, Social Services Department.

Jesson, J. (1993) 'Understanding adolescent female prostitution: A literature review.' *British Journal of Social Work* **23** (5), pp. 517–30.

Jesson, J., Luck, M., Taylor, J. (1991) *Women and HIV*. Research report for West Birmingham Health Authority, West Birmingham Health Authority Health Promotion Unit.

Jordan, B. (1996) *A Theory of Poverty and Social Exclusion*. Cambridge: Polity Press.

Joseph Rowntree Foundation (1998) *Findings – Monitoring Poverty and Social Exclusion*. York: Joseph Rowntree Foundation.

Kamenka, E. (1983) *The Portable Karl Marx*. Middlesex: Viking Penguin.

Kinnel, H. (1991) *Prostitutes' Experiences of Being in Care: Results of a Safe Project Investigation*. Birmingham Community Health Trust, Safe Project.

Lee, M., O'Brien, R. (1995) *The Game's Up: Redefining Child Prostitution*. London: The Children's Society.

Lee, R. (1993) *Doing Research on Sensitive Topics*. London: Sage.

Lee, R., Renzetti, C. (1993) 'The problem of researching sensitive topics: An introduction and overview.' In C. Renzetti and R. Lee (eds) *Researching Sensitive Topics*. London: Pluto Press.

Little, M., Kelly, S. (1998) 'A life without problems? The achievements of a therapeutic community.' In Dartington Social Research Unit, Department of Health, *Caring for Children Away from Home: Messages from Research*. Chichester: John Wiley and Sons.

Maher, L. (1995) 'In the name of love: Women and initiation to illicit drugs.' In R. Emerson Dobash, R. P. Dobash and L. Noakes (eds) *Gender and Crime*. Cardiff: University of Wales Press.

Marchant, C. (1993) 'At risk.' *Community Care*, pp. 18–19, September.

Mayall, B. (1997) 'Risky childhoods and societal responses.' *Risk and Human Behaviour Newsletter*, Issue 2, ESRC.

McKeganey, M., Barnard, M., Bloor, M., Leyland, A. (1990) 'Injecting, drug use and female street working in Glasgow.' *AIDS*, **1** (ii), pp. 1153–5.

McMullen, R. (1987) 'Youth prostitution: A balance of power.' *Journal of Adolescence*, **10** (1), pp. 35–43.

McNeish, D. (1998) 'An overview of agency views and service provision for young people abused through prostitution.' In *Whose Daughter Next? Children Abused through Prostitution*. Essex: Barnardo's.

Melrose, M. (1996) 'Enticing subjects and disembodied objects.' In H. Dean (ed.) *Ethics and Social Policy Research*. Luton: University of Luton Press in conjunction with the Social Policy Association.

Melrose, M. (1999) 'Word from the street: Reflections on the perils, pains and gender dynamics of researching "begging" in contemporary Britain.' In H. Dean (ed.) *Begging and Street Level Economic Activity*. Bristol: Policy Press.

Newman, C. (1989) *Young Runaways: Findings from Britain's First Safe House*. London: The Children's Society.

O'Connell-Davidson, J. (1995) 'The anatomy of 'free choice' prostitution.' *Gender, Work and Organization*, **2** (1), pp.1–10.

O'Connell-Davidson, J. (1998) *Prostitution, Power and Freedom*. Cambridge: Polity Press.

O'Connell-Davidson, J., Layder, D. (1994) *Methods, Sex and Madness*. London: Routledge.

O'Connell-Davidson, J., Sanchez-Taylor, J. (1996) 'Child prostitution and tourism: Beyond the stereotypes.' In J. Pilcher and S. Wagg (eds) *Thatcher's Children? Politics, Childhood and Society in the 1980's and 1990's*. London: Falmer Press.

O'Neill, M. (1994) 'Prostitution and the State: Towards a feminist practice.' In C. Lupton and T. Gillespie (eds) *Working With Violence*. Basingstoke: MacMillan.

O'Neill, M. (1997) 'Prostitute women now.' In G. Scambler and A. Scambler (eds) *Rethinking Prostitution: Purchasing Sex in the 1990's*. London: Routledge.

O'Neill, M., Goode, N., Hopkins, K. (1995) 'Juvenile prostitution: The experience of young women in residential care.' *Childright*, no. 113, pp. 14–6.

Oppenheim, C., Lister, R. (1996) 'The politics of child poverty.' In J. Pilcher and S. Wagg (eds) *Thatcher's Children? Politics, Childhood and Society in the 1980's and 1990's*. London: Falmer Press.

Patel, G. (1994) *The Porth Project: A Study of Homelessness and Running Away amongst Vulnerable Black People in Newport, Gwent.* London: The Children's Society.

Pitts, J. (1997) 'Causes of youth prostitution, new forms of practice and political responses.' In D. Barrett (ed.) *Child Prostitution in Britain: Dilemmas and Practical Responses*. London: The Children's Society.

Plant, M. (1997) 'Alcohol, drugs and social milieu.' In G. Scambler and A. Scambler (eds) *Rethinking Prostitution: Purchasing Sex in the 1990's*. London: Routledge.

Rees, G. (1993) *Hidden Truths: Young People's Experiences of Running Away*. London: The Children's Society.

Reinharz, S. (1992) *Feminist Methods in Social Research*. Oxford: Oxford University Press.

Scambler, G., Scambler, A. (1997) 'Rethinking prostitution.' In G. Scambler and A. Scambler (eds) *Rethinking Prostitution: Purchasing Sex in the 1990's*. London: Routledge.

Shaw, I., Butler, I. (1998) 'Understanding young people and prostitution: A foundation for practice?' *British Journal of Social Work*, no. 28, pp. 177–96.

Sinclair, I., Gibbs, I. (1998) *Children's Homes: A Study in Diversity*. Chichester, Wiley.

Social Exclusion Unit (1998) *Truancy and School Exclusion: Report by the Social Exclusion Unit*. Cm 3957. London: The Stationery Office.

Stein, M., Frost, N., Rees, G. (1994) *Running the Risk: Young People on the Streets of Britain Today*. London: The Children's Society.

Strauss, M. B. (1994) *Violence in the Lives of Adolescents*. New York: Norton.

Swann, S. (1998) 'A model for understanding abuse through prostitution.' In *Whose Daughter Next? Children Abused through Prostitution*. Essex: Barnardo's.

Thompson, A. (1995) 'Abuse by another name.' *Community Care*, 19–25 October 1995, pp. 16–18.

Townsend, P. (1996) *A Poor Future*. London: Lemos and Crane.

UNDP (1996) *Human Development Report 1995*. New York and Oxford: Oxford University Press.

Utting, Sir William (1997) *People like Us: The Report of the Review of the Safeguards for Children living away from Home*. London: The Stationery Office.

Van der Ploeg, J. (1989) 'Homelessness: A multidimensional problem.' *Children and Youth Services Review* **11** (1), pp. 45–62.

Wade, J., Biehal, N., Clayden, J., Stein, M. (1998) 'Going missing: Young people absent from care.' In Dartington Social Research Unit, Department of Health, *Caring for Children Away from Home: Messages from Research*. Chichester: John Wiley and Sons.

West, D. J., in association with de Villiers, B. (1992) *Male prostitution*. London: Duckworth.

Wilkinson, C. (1995) 'The drop out society.' *Young Minds Magazine*, 24.

Wilkinson, R. G. (1994) *Unfair Shares: The Effects of Widening Income Differences on the Welfare of the Young*. Essex: Barnardo's.

Wyatt, G. E., Newcomb, M., Riederle, M. (1993) *Sexual Abuse and Consensual Sex: Women's Developmental Patterns and Outcomes*. California: Sage.

THE CHILDREN'S SOCIETY
A POSITIVE FORCE FOR CHANGE

The Children's Society is one of Britain's leading charities for children and young people. Founded in 1881 as a Christian organisation, The Children's Society reaches out unconditionally to children and young people regardless of race, culture or creed.

Over 90 projects throughout England and Wales
We work with over 30,000 children of all ages, focusing on those whose circumstances have made them particularly vulnerable. We aim to help stop the spiral into isolation, anger and lost hope faced by so many young people.

We constantly look for effective, new ways of making a real difference
We measure local impact and demonstrate through successful practice that major issues can be tackled and better resolved. The Children's Society has an established track record of taking effective action: both in changing public perceptions about difficult issues such as child prostitution, and in influencing national policy and practice to give young people a better chance at life.

The Children's Society is committed to overcoming injustice wherever we find it
We are currently working towards national solutions to social isolation, lack of education and the long-term problems they cause, through focused work in several areas:

- helping parents whose babies and toddlers have inexplicably stopped eating, endangering their development;
- involving children in the regeneration of poorer communities;
- preventing exclusions from primary and secondary schools;
- providing a safety net for young people who run away from home and care;
- seeking viable alternatives to the damaging effects of prison for young offenders.

The Children's Society will continue to raise public awareness of difficult issues to promote a fairer society for the most vulnerable children in England and Wales. For further information about the work of The Children's Society or to obtain a publications catalogue, please contact:

The Children's Society, Publishing Department, Edward Rudolf House, Margery Street, London WC1X 0JL. Tel. 0171 841 4400. Fax 0171 841 4500. Website address: http://www.the-childrens-society.org.uk

The Children's Society is a registered charity: Charity Registration No. 221124.